CASUAL
POWER

CASUAL POWER

How to Power Up
Your Nonverbal Communication and
Dress Down for Success

Sherry Maysonave

Library of Congress Catalog Number: 99-73367

ISBN 1-880092-48-4

Printed in Canada

Designed by Martha Gazella-Taylor, Gazella Design
Cover design by Larry Jolly, Jolly Design
Edited by Susan Strobel

Fashion Illustrations by Barbara van den Bergh
Photography by Andrew Yates

First Edition

12 11 10 9 8 7 6 5 3 2 1

BRIGHT BOOKS

P.O. Box 50335
Austin, Texas 78763-0335
512-499-4164
Fax 512-477-9975

Acknowledgments:

Gratitude is a powerful quality, as is appreciation. I feel enchanted when I experience the rich sensations of gratitude and appreciation — although when just kept to myself, the feeling not expressed, something important seems lacking. Without acknowledging words, the ultimate power of appreciation gets short-circuited. Hence, these words of appreciation for the special people that have empowered me to write this book and to those who have made it even better.

Thank you to:

My husband, Stephen, the love of my life, for understanding how to uplift me (and so many others) by sharing your love, your many talents, and your motivational spirit — such an admirable use of your personal power. Without your love and remarkable support, *Casual Power* might never have come to fruition, or it would have taken ten times longer, and the process would have been filled with struggle. You are an incredible man.

My son, Edward Latson, for your love and unique brand of encouragement, including your inspiring letter that resides in my treasure chest.

My two daughters, Samantha Latson and Stephanie Maysonave, for your love and for always believing in me.

My mother, Thelma Wilson Horn, for planting that first seed of inspiration (your prediction that I would write a book someday) all those years ago at the Port Aransas Beach. Your prophetic words meant a lot to me; I have replayed them often, hearing your voice in my mind — especially through difficult times. And thank you for never giving me the option of slacking off when I was growing up. You taught me early on about the power of impeccable grooming and how clothing affects your results in life. Thank you for your creativity, for the thousands of hours you spent at the sewing machine on my behalf, for your unconditional love, and for believing in me.

Ann Clark, cookbook author and kitchen designer, for planting the second inspirational seed that gave birth to *Casual Power*.

Chuck Haidet, the owner of Keeper's (Exceptional Men's Apparel, Austin, Texas) for surrendering your store (store décor included) and fine fashions for the benefit of the photography for *Casual Power*.

Carol Crowsley, Image Consultant (certified by Empowerment Enterprises), for your reliability, your talent, and for working hard and sharing your calming influence during the weeks of photography sessions.

Fran Pullin, Image Consultant (certified by Empowerment Enterprises), for sharing your expertise and your beautiful clothing and accessories that enriched the photography in *Casual Power*.

Martha Gazella-Taylor of Gazella Design, Book Designer and Layout Editor for *Casual Power*, for your outstanding creative talent, for your willingness to work overtime to meet deadlines, for your integrity, and for your commitment to excellence.

Susan Strobel, Copy Editor for *Casual Power*, for your expertise with words, for your humor, for your undying attention to detail, and for not allowing me to harass the readers.

Barbara van den Bergh for your great talent as a fashion illustrator, and for your willingness to alter your designs to meet my specifications.

Andrew Yates — the best photographer — for being a pleasure to work with, even though my learning curve was high. And thanks to your team, Karen, Bonnie, and Matt, for their cooperation, patience, and smiles.

Jolly Design — Larry Jolly and Karen Luciani — for your powerful book cover design.

I dedicate this book to my amazing husband, Stephen Maysonave,
and to my dear mother, Thelma Wilson Horn.

Table of Contents

"I have wondered
how long
men would retain
their ranks
if divested
of their clothing."

— Ralph Waldo Emerson

Casual Confusion Syndrome

— CCS Strikes All IQ Levels

Deciphering today's casual dress codes is tough business. As the dress-down trend swept the business world into an unprecedented embrace, epidemic-level confusion entwined its way into the heart of professionalism. Lacking information on this new, relaxed rendition of business dress, many professionals are oblivious to the rapid speed at which they are traveling down the "Super-Sabotage Highway."

The high-technology industry — particularly the Silicon Valley — opened the door to the negotiations. And now practically all sectors of commerce are influenced by this merger of casual apparel and the workplace. Even reputedly conservative financial institutions and law firms have divorced tradition by implementing at least one casual day per week. With the conventional business suit retiring early in the week (if worn at all) — millions are suffering from **Casual Confusion Syndrome (CCS)**.

CASUAL CONFUSION SYNDROME (CCS)
Wearing casual attire inappropriately

A catchall, the word "casual" belies its carefree aura. It begets confusion. Whatever the informal occasion, two primary questions arise: How dressed down is too casual? How dressed up is not casual enough? Workplaces in most industries and social circles at all economic levels have fallen prey to this perplexing uncertainty.

Exhibiting no intellectual biases, CCS strikes all levels of intelligence — even the brilliant folks. How and why? First, let's peek into a few real-life closets and workplaces. Observe closely the subtleties as we survey a variety of dilemmas engendered by Casual Confusion Syndrome.

LONDON CONFERENCE-GOERS CAUGHT IN FOG

Packing for a week-long international banking conference held in London, Judy Shaffier, a financial executive in New York, feels perplexed by not knowing precisely what's appropriate clothing for the trip. Meanwhile, thousands of miles away, Tatsuo Matsumura, a loan officer in Tokyo, faces the same dilemma. Although travel bags await, open and empty, a reexamination of the conference information yields no clues, except for suggesting participants wear "Business Casual" attire for the daytime meetings. Anxiously surveying the contents of their closets, both Tatsuo and Judy ask, *What exactly is Business Casual?*

CEO FOUND TIED UP

After thirty years of wearing the traditional suit and tie to the office every day, Philip Meron feels exasperated. He, too, is afflicted with CCS. On Friday morning, Phil stares into his closet, stressed over what to wear. As CEO of a national health-care company, he agreed to institute one casual day a week — Friday. Yet he is afraid he will lose respect and credibility if he shows up in ordinary casual wear. Suspiciously eyeing the wash-the-car shorts, regular jeans, T-shirts, and golf garb hanging in his closet, he dons his usual navy suit and red tie, out of frustration.

As he enters the office, Phil suspects the low laughter he hears is chuckling over his predictable attire. Catching his uptight reflection in the sheen of his brass doorplate, he secretly wishes he could wow his younger cohorts with a dashing, relaxed image. If he just knew what casual garments to buy with assurance of still looking authoritative, he could enjoy the ease of dressing down for work.

Gravely threatened by CCS, Jim Ray is about to collide with casual calamity. With a devil-may-care attitude, Jim, an engineer for a technology company, hurriedly throws on a T-shirt and jeans. After tying his frayed sneakers, he glances in the mirror to admire the 49ers logo emblazoned across his shirt. Smiling at the thought of his favorite football team, he rushes on to the office.

Later that day, a meeting with a VIP client from Japan arises unexpectedly. Jim's adrenaline is pumping because the meeting concerns a multimillion-dollar deal that uses technology his team has developed — Jim's pet project. Just before the meeting begins, the VP of Marketing asks Steve, a less-senior engineer in the department, to be the technology spokesperson in the upcoming session. Outraged, Jim asks why. Jim is shocked when the VP answers that Steve, although casually dressed, looked more professional to meet with a strategic client. Wearing a collared long-sleeve shirt, dress trousers, and hard-soled shoes, Steve — not Jim — is awarded the opportunity to leap ahead in his career.

Shelia Swinson loves her job working for a national retail chain, a company that manufactures casual apparel. The relaxed atmosphere allows her creativity to flourish. Even though she has been with this company for five years, Shelia still values being employed by a large corporation that actually encourages dressing down for work. Shelia gets substantial discounts on company-made clothing, and only those labels now brush the back of her neck or tweak at her waist.

Shelia, efficient and hard working, has been particularly excited and attentive to her tasks lately. Rumors of a new higher-level position opening up in her department escalate daily. Shelia believes she is the premier candidate because her work record is excellent. She easily indulges in daydreaming about what she would do with the added prestige and power — not to mention the money.

Friday morning, Shelia's boss calls her into his office about an hour before the weekly department meeting. Her stomach flutters as she anticipates hearing good news. She is surprised to see a well-dressed young man waiting in the inner office. The butterflies in her stomach turn to wasps as Mr. Donelson introduces George as the person chosen

SILICON VALLEY ENGINEER COLLARS COLLEAGUE

HUMAN RESOURCE COORDINATOR THICKENS GLASS CEILING

to fill the new position. Brought in from another branch, George had occupied the same-level job as Shelia, at the other office. Sorely stung with disappointment, Shelia welcomes George.

Later in the day Mr. Donelson stops by to give Shelia some files to update. She brazenly asks, why George, not her? Her boss replies that, while her work was excellent, the overall level of Shelia's professionalism was not on par with what the company rewarded with high-level promotion.

Swallowing hard, Shelia sits stunned. Even though the company manufactures casual apparel and encourages casual dress, Shelia is not perceived as ambitious or highly professional — not because of her work record, but because of her overly casual image.

Dress is a powerful business tool. Whether you are dressed down or up, this fact cannot be overlooked if you aspire to go beyond your current level of success. Did any of these anecdotes — all real-life incidents — hit a chord with you? Be sure to note which ones and why.

As a business-image consultant for a wide range of industries, I have often found clients to be confused about casual attire. Common to all hierarchies of business, Casual Confusion Syndrome operates in full force at many Fortune 500 companies, from the CEO down to the lowest rung on the corporate ladder. Small businesses are no exception. Owners and employees at all pay scales are puzzled about how to balance professionalism with casual attire.

HOW DID WE GET SO CASUALLY CONFUSED?

For starters, the words "casual days" or "dressing down" for the workplace were foreign to the printed page until the early 1990s. Until then, in business, casual apparel was appropriate only in blue-collar, labor-intensive industries. Unlike the continually changing fashion sphere, major changes in business dress almost always correspond with an important event or trend in the world. Technological advancements have changed our ways of doing business. At the same time, Total Quality Management emphasized empowering and valuing the employee. Companies encouraged dressing down, hoping to increase employee morale and productivity.

A lack of precedent for the concept of "Business Casual" dress explains in part the perplexity surrounding this new paradigm. Never in the history of U.S. business has casual apparel permeated so many industries as now; never has the application of technology tools governed business as today.

A glimpse into the American professional-dress archives, from the early 1900s to the present, sheds more light on how business fashions have changed with major world events and trends.

■ At the beginning of the twentieth century, we find that professional dress was greatly affected by the Industrial Revolution. To be set apart and to maximize authority over their blue-collar machinists, industrialists intentionally wore dressier apparel. In the early 1900s executive office, the three-piece suit reigned — matching jacket, vest, trousers. Add a white shirt, with heavily starched collar and cuffs, and a short necktie or bowtie to envision the typical manager's uniform of that time.

■ Business fashions in the Prohibition era (1920-1933) were characterized by double-breasted, wide-lapeled suits. Often associated with the flourishing organized-crime scene, the dapper double-breasted suit remained strong into the 1930s. Extra-wide ties added breadth to macho chests as men continued to dominate the business world.

■ Early in 1940, thousands of women entered the business workforce as men were called to military duty. In 1945, at the end of World War II, the surviving men were our national heroes. Inspired by the uniform of the war veterans, the gray flannel suit — British cut with matching vest — held sway as the most stylish look for professional men and women of the '50s.

■ The Vietnam War and the anti-authority flower children of the '60s influenced customary fashions with earthy styles, and tie-dyed and psychedelic-patterned fabrics. Still, the three-piece suit remained the Establishment's standard for serious business.

■ The mid-'70s cold-war conformity underscored the subtle embodiment of power. A navy pin-striped suit, white shirt, foulard tie, red in background with tiny navy chevrons or some other small print — completed the ultimate power outfit of the period. IBM, also called "Big Blue" or "The Winged-Tipped Warrior," and *Dress for Success* author John Malloy helped dictate professional style and dress codes.

A business woman in this era also wore a dark navy suit: a mid-calf skirt topped with a matching blazer-type suit jacket of conventional cut, with small lapels. A crisp white blouse with a small ribbon tie at the neck — red or a red-toned color like burgundy — completed the female power suit for the '70s.

■ With gridiron battles nationally enshrined, 1980 styles augmented the '70s power look with widely extended shoulder pads. Exaggerated broad shoulders gained the edge for both sexes.

■ The Information Age of the '90s downsized and expanded traditional ways of conducting business. Personal computers, e-mail, fax machines, cellular phones, voice mail, and the Internet all facilitate conducting business from anywhere on the globe. The push of a button brings worldwide business transactions directly into bedrooms, tanning salons, bathrooms, cars, gyms — anywhere one chooses to be. This flexibility gave rise to satellite offices and an increase in the number of home offices. The "virtual corporation" concept became commonplace as long-term employment was often exchanged for consulting contracts.

Aftershock ripples from this data-based earthquake in the business world have clearly shifted the professional-dress paradigm. The frenetic, ever-changing pace of the Information Age demands the flexibility of casual wear. Except for those who tamed unexplored territory — winning the Wild, Wild West — casual clothes have never had a place in an executive office. Even on the frontier, wearing informal dress was based on dealing with nature's elements and survival. Casual wear has never enjoyed the status it does today. More importantly, we have never exhibited such casual ignorance.

To be successful today, a person must be able to dress casually and still exude as much power, credibility, and authority as when wearing a traditional business suit. This is a tall order, considering that casual wear typically consists of separate, self-contained articles of informal clothing, none of which come with instructions on how to assemble them into a professional outfit. With all this talk of relaxing the dress code, casual wear is supposed to be *easier*. Ironically, traditional suits and their accessories are far less complicated. Anyone, male or female, can put on a well-tailored suit and instantly look more professional and powerful.

Just as our technological world is more complex, today's business arena requires style skills that surpass those we use when choosing a suit. The challenge is how to create a powerful, pulled-together image using individual garments made of various fabrics. Our purpose in this book is to show how to dress casually and still command respect and exude professionalism, authority, and personal power — even when dressed in coordinates.

In their clonelike uniformity, dark business suits offer a type of armoring and refuge that is not possible with casual wear. Dress-down days or casual dress codes remove the protective wrappings, revealing the true nature of an individual. In the previous case history, when I interviewed Shelia Swinson, she admitted to being lazy about her professional image. She allowed her mind to emphasize that she worked for a company that manufactured and sold weekend-type casual apparel. Thus, Shelia experienced no internal conflict with her indolent attitude about her professional attire. She willed herself into believing that she was judged strictly on her performance. Even though Shelia was a dedicated, diligent employee, the energies she directed to her career image did not match her zeal for success. She could have enjoyed the comforts of dressing down and still have presented a potent businesslike image in power-casual apparel. Perhaps then she would know the satisfaction of being in George's shoes.

Casual wear appropriate for the business arena scarcely resembles the clothing suitable for washing your car or weekend lounging. One would think that working adults would naturally grasp this concept; nonetheless, gross misinterpretation of Business Casual dress remains alarmingly common. Individuals and corporations risk credibility, respect, and profits with their flagrant misconceptions of how to dress down and maintain a professional image.

Your choices of dress-down attire reflect directly your respect for your workplace, your career goals, and your level of overall professionalism.

When dressed down, do you show up as a *real* professional in your workplace? Or are *you* afflicted with Casual Confusion Syndrome? Are you aware if this problem has snared you — even sometimes — in its perplexing web? Let's find out with the following yes-or-no questionnaire. Take some time to honestly reflect upon your answers or feelings that arise.

ARE YOU AFFLICTED WITH CASUAL CONFUSION SYNDROME?

- Do you ever experience even the slightest bit of confusion or frustration regarding your casual apparel? In your workplace? In your closet? While shopping?
- Are you perplexed by social invitations that suggest casual attire, wondering just **how casual** the host/hostess intends?
- Does your casual wardrobe consist mainly of gym clothes, T-shirts, and jeans, with nothing or little else in between those items and your business suits?
- Are you ever embarrassed because you misinterpreted the degree of casual appropriate for the occasion and so you underdressed? Or overdressed?
- Do your choices for dress-down days ever keep you from meeting with a client, a prospect, or a superior in your workplace? Have your choices embarrassed you?
- Have you ever apologized for being too casually dressed? Have you ever wanted to apologize? In your workplace? Socially?
- Do you think only of jeans and khakis for your workplace casual attire?

If you answered "yes" to *any* of the above questions, you definitely show disturbing symptoms. Banish the thought that you are too smart or too well bred for CCS to affect *you*. Neither intelligence nor breeding is a factor in keeping CCS at bay. CCS strikes people of all levels of intelligence, in all classes of society. Far from being alone, you are one of millions.

THE SIX PRIMARY CAUSES OF EPIDEMIC-LEVEL CASUAL CONFUSION:

1. The concept of casual attire in a business setting just recently became popular and accepted in the early 1990s. Company policy makers wrongly assumed that the differences between workplace-casual and casual-lounging attire were clearly understood by everyone.

Dressing down for work existed in Silicon Valley in the '80s, but outside of high-tech companies, the practice was not widespread. From 1992 to 1995, studies show a 43 percent increase in the number of companies that adopted casual days or casual dress codes. Casual attire has now replaced traditional business dress at least one day a week for 90 percent of U.S. office workers, with over 55 percent dressing down daily for work. Both numbers continue to climb. Training concerning this new style of business dress is sorely lacking.

2. Casual wear typically consists of separate, self-contained articles of clothing in varying fabrics — none of which come with outfit assembly instructions.

Traditional business suits and their accessories are far less complicated than putting together separate garments for an overall respectable, professional outfit.

3. Workplace dress codes are fraught with unclear guidelines and glaring ambiguities.

When there are no clear, specific rules, people tend to seek the lowest common denominator. An enormous range of "looks" emcompasses casual attire. The absence of guidance and education invites poor judgment. Even with the best intentions, personal interpretation of Business Casual dress rarely aligns with spoken or unspoken company ideals.

Sanctioning casual attire with zero guidelines opens the door for excessively casual apparel to enter. And enter it will. A total lack of professional-dress guidelines or unclear rules creates and encourages self-destructive dynamics. In my consulting work with corporations, I have found poorly written dress codes and unspoken rules to be such a gigantic problem that the next entire chapter of this book is devoted to exploring and unraveling casual sabotage for the individual.

4. Mixed messages about casual dress bombard us daily.

Successful people in the public eye exhibit contrasting fashion personalities and styles of working. The original birthday suit of one of the world's richest men, technology bigwig Bill Gates, was surely casual. Conversely, San Francisco's prominent mayor, Willie Brown, was just as surely born in formal wear — at the least, a Brioni suit, cufflinks, and expensive lace-up shoes. Microsoft has a comprehensive casual-dress policy while Mayor Brown has outlawed all casual days for City Hall employees.

Presidential candidates have been criticized for appearing stuffy and unapproachable in their power suits and power ties. Yet critics tear at their seams should a candidate dare to show up without a tie, or wearing a turtleneck or a leather jacket. Successful CEOs can appear on talk shows and ads wearing the same turtleneck and get rave reviews.

Magazine ads commonly portray tank tops (with spaghetti straps), or unbuttoned shirts, worn tails out with low-slung jeans — as the ultimate dressed-down look full of sexual prowess. Yet unless these styles are worn only in private life, more than hands may get shaken.

5. The huge selection of fashions in the stores bewilders even the shopping savvy.

Our consumer society loves choices. Yet the huge inventories of clothing displayed in today's retail scene contributes heavily to dress-down dilemmas. Most of us feel overwhelmed when we are shopping for clothing. Quite often we go into sensory overload from the profuse display of brands, styles, fabrics, and colors. When our senses are over-stimulated with too many distinctions to make at one time, part of our brain literally shuts down. At the least, judgment gets fuzzy. Add this condition to the lack of clarity about what is appropriate casual wear for business, and we have a problem: Arriving back home from shopping with unsuitable clothing can sabotage us professionally.

Retailers and manufacturers are smart to cash in on this new development in business dress. Their promotional efforts reflect smart marketing, but one inherent problem exists: Not all designers, manufacturers, retailers, and salespeople are accurately informed about what constitutes empowering, professional casual wear for conducting successful business in all industries. More importantly, many salespeople are often ill-informed about what clothing works for your particular body type and your personal goals. A clothing item or an entire outfit may be advertised as "Friday's Dressing" type apparel, or may be displayed in the "Career" section, or could sport a label, *Executive Casual Wear.* None of these marketing manuevers guarantees that the garment or outfit is appropriate for the workplace or that it is empowering for you. Other chapters of this book deal with effective shopping techniques, including body type and budget concerns.

6. **The word "casual" fosters confusion. It demands to be decoded.** Casual dress represents more than just one category of attire. Six classifications of informal dress have been incorrectly lumped together as *"casual."* Failure to recognize and understand the nuances of these categories lays the foundation for the widespread confusion that exists today.

A diverse range of garments and accessories is represented within these six primary classifications: Shoes could mean hiking boots, sneakers, sandals, loafers, or high heels, for example. And a casual jacket could mean a fine wool blazer or a ski parka.

These six categories make up casual dress: **Active Casual, Rugged Casual, Sporty Casual, Smart Casual, Dressy Casual, and Business Casual.** The names may vary according to where you live: Rugged Casual is sometimes called *Outdoorsy Casual,* Smart Casual may be called *Snappy Casual,* and Dressy Casual may be referred to as *Casual Elegance.* With everything from jogging shorts to sport coats and ties all being referred to as dressing down, it isn't surprising that CCS runs rampant in our society.

Are you casually informed or informally confused?

THE SIX CLASSIFICATIONS OF INFORMAL DRESS

- Active Casual
- Rugged Casual
- Sporty Casual

- Smart Casual
- Dressy Casual
- Business Casual

Take note, the *"Grunge"* look is *not* listed as a category and will never be in my book. Grunge is actually subzero, below the line of even the most casual attire to wear publicly. If forced to give it a label, I would call it *Slob Casual.* This is not a category of clothing, but a mindset. If this is how you usually dress, it is time for *you* to grow up. Consistent grunge in the adult world earmarks you as frozen in adolescence. The middle schools of America are filled with adolescents in grunge clothing, the only place this fad can begin to make the grade.

Escape being a victim of Casual Confusion Syndrome. CCS has a cure! The first step toward "**Casual Enlightenment**" is to strengthen

FIG. 1:1   UNISEX ACTIVE CASUAL WEAR

your ability to differentiate between the categories of dressed-down attire. To help you develop this skill, let's take a look at six scenarios outside the workplace that require informal clothing and identify which specific Casual category applies. Then we will delve into the nuances of Business Casual dress.

SCENARIO I

You meet friends for cappucino after working out in the gym, running, rollerblading, biking, playing tennis, racquetball, golf — any sport of your choice. The appropriate clothing for these activities clearly indicates that you have been *physically active*. This type of casual wear is called **Active Casual.**

Jogging suits, warm-ups, wind suits, running shorts, tennis skirts, biking shorts, leggings, leotards, snow-ski garb, etc. exemplify this classification. With the exception of *some* golf clothing, Active Casual has NO business in the workplace.

FIG. 1:2   MORE UNISEX ACTIVE CASUAL WEAR

Scenario 2

It's Saturday and brrr, it's cold! You are helping friends move some antique furniture from storage, and you will have lunch together while you are out. You have chosen to wear your heavy socks and a hiking-type boot, a flannel shirt with jeans or heavy khakis, a camouflage shirt, or a sweater — topped with an insulated parka. You are dressed in **Rugged Casual** attire.

The *Rugged Casual* category draws garments from the typical apparel of the more outdoorsy sports, like hunting, fishing, backpacking, rock climbing, etc. Unless your job is related to these types of industries, this apparel does not mean *business* in the workplace.

FIG. I:3   UNISEX RUGGED CASUAL WEAR

FIG. I:4   MORE EXAMPLES OF UNISEX RUGGED CASUAL WEAR

Scenario 3A

It's your day off. You are running errands, going for a massage, just generally hanging out. Let's say you are wearing cotton pants, shorts, or jeans, a heavyweight T- or sweat shirt, a button-down or polo style shirt, a belt, and tennis shoes. This type of casual is called **Sporty Casual.**

Anytime you are wearing a sneaker-type shoe with jeans, khakis, walking shorts, skirts, etc., and you are **not** participating in a sport, you are dressed in the **Sporty Casual** category. Notice, it is sport-**y**. Most sports have particular items of clothing that support participants in performing well in that game. This category is not about playing a sport, but more about the relaxed look of a spectator. *Sportswear* has been synonymous with casual separates in the fashion world for years. Since that term was coined over fifty years ago, the world has changed dramatically. Today, the *sportswear* section of a store includes everything except suits, dresses, and formal wear.

FIG. 1:5 MALE SPORTY CASUAL WEAR

FIG. 1:6 FEMALE SPORTY CASUAL WEAR

Scenario 3B

To be really clear on the **Sporty Casual** casual category, let's take a look at another scenario. It's Saturday midday. You're meeting some friends for a burger and then to catch a movie at your local theater. You are wearing clothing similar to what was described in the previous scenario of **Sporty Casual**, minus the sneaker-type shoe. In this scene, your shoe is soft-soled, but it is not a sneaker. You are still **Sporty Casual**.

FIG. I:7 MALE SPORTY CASUAL WEAR

FIG. I:8 FEMALE SPORTY CASUAL WEAR

Sporty Casual reeks of "ordinary" casualness — your clothing is not slovenly, but it is not as pulled-together or as chic as in the following categories.

SCENARIO 4

You are going to an informal dinner with friends in an upscale restaurant. If male, you are wearing dress trousers (or even crisp jeans*), a long-sleeve shirt, maybe a tie, leather loafers or dressy slip-ons, patterned socks or solid-colored dress socks, a tipped belt, and you may or may not wear a sport coat. You are dressed in the **Smart Casual** category.

*If you are wearing crisp jeans, you must wear a sport coat for *Smart Casual*.

FIG. I:9 FEMALE SMART CASUAL OUTFIT

If female, you are wearing slacks, crisp jeans, or a skirt (long or short), a blouse or turtleneck, a fashionable belt, a jacket, a vest, or a sweater coordinated to your outfit, hosiery or socks with boots, flats (leather, suede, or fabric) or mid-heel shoes, and jewelry, such as earrings that complement your overall outfit, at least. You are dressed in the **Smart Casual** category. Again, if you are wearing jeans, wearing a jacket upgrades you to *Smart Casual*. This category demands a pulled-together, harmonious, complete look with colors, fabrics, shoes, and accessories, for both men and women.

FIG. I:10 *female smart casual outfit*

FIG. I:11 MALE SMART CASUAL OUTFIT

FIG. I:12 *male smart casual outfit*

SCENARIO 5

FIG. I:I3 FEMALE DRESSY CASUAL OUTFIT

You are going to an art gallery exhibit on opening night, and then to dinner with friends. The invitation suggested "Casual Attire." Due to the nature and the time of the event, the host means **Dressy Casual (Casual Elegance)**, which is similar to Smart Casual, with *no jeans*.

For male or female, the shoes take on a dressier tone, and the fabrics are richer, dressier. For women, this level of casual implies a pant suit, a dress, or coordinated separates in semi-dressy fabrics. *Dressy Casual* demands that the outfit be well-coordinated and accessorized.

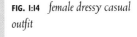

FIG. I:I4 *female dressy casual outfit*

For men, this category indicates dress trousers, turtleneck or mock-turtle version, a dress shirt or a silk sport shirt (long-sleeved), a tie (optional), and a jacket or sport coat.

Casual weddings call for this type of attire, as well. Out of respect for the ceremonial nature of a wedding, a *dressy* dressed-down look is required, regardless of location, when casual attire is requested.

FIG. I:I5 MALE DRESSY CASUAL OUTFIT

FIG. I:I6 *male dressy casual outfit*

A SIMPLE DEFINITION OF BUSINESS CASUAL:

"A comfortably relaxed version of classic business attire, with no sacrifice of professionalism or personal power."

FIG. 1:17 *female business casual outfit*

Business Casual is only one category of business attire. Business dress has three primary categories: Power Business, General Business, and Business Casual. While Business Casual attire is a recent addition to traditional business dress, human resources experts claim that it is here to stay as a permanent fixture in corporate America.

Business Casual draws from the *Smart Casual* and *Dressy Casual* categories, with many distinctions. True Business Casual attire incorporates the more tailored garments from those two classifications.

Active and *Rugged Casual* clothing is clearly *not* businesslike, unless you work as a tennis pro or a personal trainer, or in the outdoors like a professional fly-fisherman. The apparel of *Sporty Casual* falls short of embodying professional attitudes. Intended for other use, Sporty Casual attire fails to command enough power and respect for a full-tilt Business Casual look in a public meeting.

Dressing down for business has begun to assume global proportions. Professionals in the U.K., France, Italy, Germany, Spain, Mexico, and many other countries are following America's lead and are beginning to relax their business dress codes. In London, one of the most conservative financial climates in the world, some banks have instituted a weekly casual Friday. Japan remains formal, however, I predict a short lag time before we see business dress relax there as well. When they are certain of their understanding and of their ability to do it correctly, the Japanese will loosen their formality in business attire, at the appropriate times.

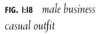

FIG. 1:18 *male business casual outfit*

Empowering Business Casual apparel is shown in detail in Chapters 5 and 6. If you want to fully understand this classification of business dress, don't skip a single page in this book. Abundant rewards await you, professionally and personally.

Each of the six casual categories can look a thousand ways with varying garments. Opt for a contemporary look or choose classic versions. Within the parameters of each category, one can also dress in a festive or glitzy party mode. Variations also occur according to the taste of the individual wearer and the condition of the garments. Rumpled anything downgrades *you*. So does soiled, torn, tired, or cheap. There is always a smart-*er* look one can aspire to within each division of casual attire.

No need to obsess over the clothing pieces listed with these classifications. The above examples were used just to help you begin making basic observations and distinctions about the differing degrees of casual dress. This is an essential step in grasping the important nuances of *Business Casual*. You can then consciously select casual garments for your business wardrobe that are multipurpose and fill other wardrobe needs, and garments that work hard for you on the job.

Whatever your task, the right tool makes it faster and easier. A food processor dices onions in seconds, but this simple action takes mega-minutes with the usual kitchen knife. A power lawn mower reduces grass cutting time by half or more over using a push mower to blade the identical lawn. A blender can whirl ice into tasty margaritas or smoothies in seconds, but ice melts before it can be shaved by hand.

Dentists, surgeons, chefs, architects, and plumbers all require distinct tools to do their jobs well and efficiently. Whatever your profession, your business image is one of your fundamental tools. Just as potent as your PC, empowering clothing can catapult you to the fast track. Are you *consciously* using your clothing and grooming — especially when dressed down — as valuable business assets and high-powered tools to propel you toward greater success?

YOUR IMAGE IS A POWERFUL BUSINESS TOOL!

What is the most impressive power tool you own or use on a regular basis?
The Internet?
Automatic spellcheck?
E-mail?
Fax?
Your sonar toothbrush?

"A man
becomes
a creature
of his uniform."

— Napoleon I

2

Are You a Business Casual Casualty?

Have you dressed down...*down-down-down* to conduct your business? Are you crippling your future by presently dressing down *too* far on casual days? If you are consistently wearing excessively relaxed attire, you could be on your way to becoming a business fatality statistic: a terminal victim of the **Casual Confusion Syndrome.**

Whether you are a CEO, or in sales, management, marketing, engineering, or administration, or you are self-employed, business casual dress will touch your world. A take-me-seriously business image shows versatility with appropriate casual wear, yet consistently strikes a highly professional profile.

The work environment demands a certain level of professionalism at all times. You are the face of your business in the world — your company personified — and the mirror of your own future — right now, today. To be identified as a major league player and to be taken seriously in today's game of business, *you* must take your casual apparel seriously. Business is a game. How are you playing it? Are you wearing the appropriate gear?

Every game, every sport has particular attire and equipment designed to support the players in performing well and to protect them from injury. What would happen to an NFL quarterback who resented wearing the heavy shoulder and thigh pads, the rigid protective cup, the bulky helmet, and the face guard, and decided to play without them? His career would be over the first game he attempted to play without these game necessities.

Apparel necessities exist for playing the game of business just as for sports. Granted, no quarterback in his right mind would leave his body unprotected with 300-pound tackles coming at him. But is comfort important to you? In my consulting work, I have heard preposterous comments from men and women regarding their expected comfort level in business clothing. Some demand that their streetwear feel as comfortable as their bathrobes. Yes, comfort is central to an authentic professional image. Ease and comfort are the outgrowth of proper fit and quality fabrics.

Equally important is the expression of your individuality. No one wants to be a uniformed clone or a corporate robot. As Robert Pante said, *"Don't look like a filing cabinet!"* Expressed appropriately, individualism in professional dress operates as a people magnet. Still, if you take too many liberties with your self-expression and your comfort in your business game attire, it is you who will lose in the end.

Currently, in your dress-down attire, are you exercising the freedom to express yourself with a look that attracts wins and success to you? Or are you a distraction, making it difficult to win easily? **Distractions hold enormous negative power.** Others cannot hear what you have to say when your physical appearance disturbs and distracts their focus. Chatter inside their mind is activated, dominating their thoughts. In the next chapter the nonverbal communication aspects of business dress are discussed in more depth.

Consistently wearing slob attire in the workplace erodes your self-respect and confidence. What's more, it diminishes your professionalism in the eyes of your cohorts, your superiors, and your clients. If your coworkers always see you sloppily attired and groomed, then that image of you becomes the way they think of you as a *whole*.

What about "eroding self-respect"? How can that be? We internalize our usual exterior image as the truth about our whole being. When you consistently see yourself in the mirror, dressed like a slob, your psyche

CASUAL DAYS ARE NEVER LICENSED SLOB DAYS.

absorbs that you are a slob. Even if you avoid mirrors, this remains true. Your eyes — and your entire body — take in the sight and feeling of what you are wearing at all times. Your subconscious mind silently records detailed information about your actual garments, their condition and fabric quality. If you wear shabby attire, you may as well be playing a subliminal tape that repeatedly bombards your psyche with negative thoughts like: *"I am a lazy slob. Sloppy, tacky clothes are all I deserve. I am a loser."*

The subconscious mind is one of the most sensitive, powerful instruments in the universe. It magnifies and expands whatever it internalizes, whatever is impressed upon it through image or feeling. If you customarily present yourself as a slob in the workplace, you are heading down a grim career path. If the freedom to dress casually has allowed you to indulge a slob tendency, then you are on the road to becoming more and more slovenly with yourself, with your work ethic, with your career — with your life. As Aristotle said, *"We are what we repeatedly do."*

Your current dress-down habits supply the cement that is now paving your future career path. You can play the game to win, increasing your future options, or you can play to just get by, inflating obstacles and formidable roadblocks.

Listed below are some dress-down specifics that are *not* acceptable for playing the game of business in most industries. To win at the game of business, to succeed beyond your current level, avoid these casual "no-no's" in the workplace — at all costs. The items on this list do not score in the game. Wearing these items places you at risk of stalling out and going no farther than you are right now — a Business Casual Casualty.

(More information on each of these items can be found in the illustrated sabotage section later in this chapter.)

ARE YOU SABOTAGING YOURSELF WITH THESE BUSINESS CASUAL "NO-NO'S"?

- T-shirt and jeans (worn together)
- Dirty sneakers
- Sandals
- No belt (and your pants have belt loops)
- Shirttail out

- Caps (baseball)
- Active wear (jogging suits, wind suits, warm-ups, etc.)
- Poorly coordinated outfits
- Humorous attire or accessories
- Leggings or stirrup pants

- Sleeveless attire
- No hosiery or no socks
- Shorts
- Rugged outdoor wear (Camouflage fabrics, military fatigues, insulated parkas or vests, hiking boots, etc.)

Some of you are declaring, *"Everyone in my workplace wears these things. Everybody dresses down like this!"* Yes, I am sure that some do. If you join them, will it get you ahead? I remember the tactic my children used on me: *"But, Mom, e-v-e-r-y-one is wearing that; everybody is going there!"* We all have a need to belong, to fit in; such is human nature. Unfortunately, we often choose to blend in instead of reaching for our dreams of success.

Are you *consciously* dressing down for success or are you *unconsciously* dressing down for sabotage? Has your personal saboteur taken over your career goals? Most of us battle the personal saboteur at some point. A sly intelligent force, the personal saboteur is an aspect of the human psyche that can negatively influence our clothing choices to undermine our success. It can function at varying levels. To uncover the extreme subtlety of how their personal saboteur was operating, many of my clients had to don scuba gear. On the other hand, some of my clients easily found that their personal saboteur was a murderer in their life — a serial killer!

If you are not achieving your goals, or if you have no goals, a personal saboteur is working behind the scenes to trip you, to hold you back from success. Your personal saboteur can behave as a monster. I named mine McSly, after I learned to laugh at its clever pranks.

The instant you open your closet door to decide what to wear, McSly engages you in dialogue. McSly authoritatively informs you that today dressing down means extremely relaxed apparel, the sloppy grunge look. Suddenly, a compulsion to wear your rattiest casual clothing overcomes you. Certain that you feel miraculously better in them, you surrender to the feeling. Sounding just like your own thoughts, McSly's voice echoes in your head: *"You know you function best when you are r-e-a-l-l-y comfortable. And, of course, only your well-worn knock-around clothes are truly comfortable. Oh, who cares anyway? It's casual day, and everybody will dress way down. Don't tuck your shirt in or wear those hard-soled shoes today! No one cares! It doesn't matter!"*

Then there are the times when you have decided on a decent outfit, but you notice a loose or missing button, a slight tear, a few soiled spots, wrinkles, or unpolished shoes. You might hear McSly proclaiming: *"No one will notice!"*

Do you have a McSly living casually in your closet?

McSly has the astonishing ability to accompany you wherever you may go — especially shopping. Often functioning as your Chief Advisor for Career Apparel, McSly encourages you to purchase cheap fabrics and unflattering, unprofessional clothing. McSly resists buying quality dress-down apparel. McSly does not want you to win big in life. McSly's job is to make certain that your confidence is undermined and your good-looks potential stays untapped.

True to the saboteur nature, McSly is happiest when *you* look inappropriate, unsuccessful, and unappealing. McSly's cunning ways inspire you to make poor shopping selections, deliberately steering you clear of anything resembling a wardrobe plan. Then, when you find yourself inappropriately dressed, McSly shrieks *"See, I told you! You are an imbecile slob! You have subzero class!"*

We all have one of these gremlins residing in the darkest closet of our mind, the subconscious. McSly is just a part of you. It cannot be removed, but it is trainable. For starters, take note of the running commentary inside your mind about clothing in general — yours, other people's, dress codes, the shopping process, etc. Most importantly, increase your awareness of your *willingness* to present yourself in the most attractive, powerful way when you dress casually. This will require some probing into *your* deeper feelings.

Our goal is to examine some of your more conscious attitudes and to illuminate some of your unconscious beliefs. The subconscious aspects of our psyches influence, drive, and control us to an extraordinary degree. It is prudent to take a look and discover just what course you are on.

To find out, answer the questions below. Be forewarned that your personal saboteur will encourage you to fudge on the truth. Get a pen and paper to jot down your answers. Subconscious responses are more readily accessible if you immediately record what spontaneously comes up, **without censoring.** Relax. Note your feelings and thoughts as you contemplate each question. Write single words, phrases, or whatever pops into your mind. Don't screen or alter your natural responses. It can be fun and amusing to discover what you may have been McSlyishly hiding from yourself!

1. What kind of thoughts and feelings do you experience when you spend money on your clothing? Is shopping with a plan or specific budget for your traditional business clothes foreign to you? How about your Business Casual clothing? Do you have a dollar ceiling to pay for a casual garment? How much?

2. Do you insist that all your casual apparel be washable? Do you resent spending money to send your casual clothes to a quality laundry or dry cleaner?

3. When do you think through the events of your workday? In the morning, do you tumble out of bed, hit the shower, absentmindedly throw on the nearest clean (dirty?) clothes, and think about your schedule while on your way to work or after you get to the office? Do unexpected events on casual days find you dressed down-*down-down*, too inappropriately to handle business properly? How often? Have you ever been passed over for promotions or special assignments?

4. How comfortable are you with people who are well dressed and powerful? (Rate your degree of comfort on a scale from 1 to 10 with 1 being very uncomfortable and 10 being very comfortable.) What do you think and feel when this happens? What do you think about them? (Do you label them as slick, snobby, etc.?) What do you think about yourself? Do you ever experience a feeling of physical shrinking or a desire to back away from them? Do you ever feel personally diminished or "less than"?

5. Do you ever avoid meeting that unexpected client or coworker because you are dressed down *too* far to make a businesslike impression? Do you feel that you have to explain or apologize for your attire? How often? Under what circumstances? Do you have regretful thoughts about your clothing choices for the day? Have you ever intentionally eluded the boss because of your appearance? Do you delay meetings or change meeting places, restaurants, etc. due to your clothing? Do you ever decline invitations, or avoid certain people, places, jobs, or businesses because you are too casually attired?

6. When you catch that unexpected glimpse of yourself in the mirror, how happy are you with your reflection? (Rate on a scale from 1 to 10 with 1 being very unhappy and 10 being very happy.) Are you ever

surprised that your reflection does not look like the person you perceive yourself to be? Do you ever have a sinking feeling or wonder what on earth possessed you to buy or wear those particular garments? Do you purposefully avoid mirrors, even if it means extra steps?

7.   Have you refused to get on the dress-down bandwagon? Although informed of a casual work-related event, do you wear your regular business suit anyway because you don't have anything else to wear or you don't know what else to wear? Or both? Do you have only jeans and shorts for casual wear?

Any surprise answers? Take a few moments to reflect upon your responses and their implications. How many times did you answer Yes? Tally them up and find out your level of personal saboteur activity.

SABOTEUR ACTIVITY SCALE

1 to 3	Beware, Saboteur activity is likely. Watch for subtle caution signs on your career roadway. You may be BCCP, a Business Casual Casualty in Progress.
4 to 5	Sound the Personal Saboteur Warning. There is a stop sign, a red light ahead on your career path. You are definitely BCCP!
6 or more	**Personal Saboteur Alarm!** There is a serial killer, at large! You are beyond BCCP. Look for your name on the Endangered Species list. Your personal saboteur may be happily writing your career epitaph at this moment.

If you are feeling righteous, or if you are justifying your way of dressing, or if your mind is chirping on and on about the questions you just answered — guess what. Your very own gremlin is in charge and hard at work. When light is shed on the activities of the personal saboteur, there are some predictable behavior patterns. McSly may come on stronger with inner dialogue, denying new awareness or information. Anyone else who is giving you this information is also wrong. *"What do they know, right?"* Just notice the McSlyish chatter and chuckle to yourself that you have the opportunity to get better acquainted with your personal saboteur.

Consider any discovery about your thoughts, feelings, or habits to be a big win and a giant step toward taming your personal saboteur.

Another tactic your personal saboteur may take is to go underground, to regroup and return with new subtleties to sabotage the changes you are considering. If, for instance, you think *"Well, gee, I would love to look great all the time, but there is no way I can afford it. It takes megabucks, too bad I am not rich."* That is the personal saboteur still throwing you curveballs. It is absolutely untrue that it takes a money tree to be well dressed. Yes, abundant cash flow makes it easier. Nonetheless, by planning and learning to make good choices, you can dress well consistently and stay within your budget. (See Chapter 8 for more detail.)

You may think that you cannot look good until you lose some pounds. This is nonsense (and most assuredly a trick of your saboteur). Of course, just as having lavish funds makes it easier to look fabulous, so does having a trim figure. Studies do show that people who carry excess weight have to work harder to be perceived as professional. However, if you are using your size as an excuse, watch out! McSly is feeding you sabotaging falsehoods to keep you from the benefits of a professional image. Regardless of your extra weight, you can present yourself in a powerful, more attractive way — today.

Unfortunately, your personal saboteur does not restrict its range to wardrobe concerns. Honoring no boundaries or sacred territories, that same inner dynamic can set you up for repeated failure in other areas of your life. Using deft rationalization, it schemes to have you engage in activities you are not proud of, then ridicules you as the inevitable consequences ensue. From talking with many clients about this phenomenon, I have heard about many fascinating McSly episodes.

THE CASE OF TOM

One of my regular clients gave his brother, Tom, the birthday present of an initial consultation with me. Tom would never have booked an appointment on his own; he was entrenched in a sloppy mode of dressing for work and was proud of it. Tom came reluctantly — and only because of the gift certificate. When arranging the appointment, he actually asked if he could redeem the certificate for money. His brother had warned me this might happen, so I refused.

In our session, Tom openly displayed hostility and resentment for people who dressed as if clothes mattered. He scoffed at my suggestions for wardrobe and grooming changes, reeling off hundreds of philosophies (excuses) why he would not change. Tom was stuck in a '60s, Old Hippie mentality. His interest and curiosity did pick up when I talked about the incongruency of his professional goals with his current appearance. His brother had confided that Tom was quite talented but frustrated in his job. Speaking frankly, I told him that I detected personal saboteur activity in his rebellion against a professional image. Giving him a "Saboteur Handout" from my files, I urged him to take a deeper look at his attitudes.

Much to my surprise, Tom did some soul searching about his rebellious attitudes about fine clothing. In particular, he looked at his resentment of the quality attire worn by the upper executives of his company. Although these feelings had been unacknowledged until now, he realized that — regardless of his salary — he always seemed to struggle with his budget. Truthfully, he could never seem to afford the kind of clothes they wore. Adding fuel to the fire, Tom had been reprimanded for his slipshod image in his evaluations each year.

When Tom honestly explored his rebellion about dressing professionally, he was astonished. He realized there was a connection to the very same saboteur dynamic that caused him to run short of money every month. His McSly sneakily created ongoing financial stress by urging him to spend beyond his means on insignificant items, things he didn't even really want. At the same time, it verbally beat him to a pulp inside with *"See, I told you. You are a rotten, lousy money manager. You are scum. You will never succeed at anything! Just look at you!"*

Tom had resisted taking a higher position in his company because he did not want to wear a suit and tie on a daily basis — or so he had consciously rationalized. Actually, there was an unconscious, fear-based mistrust of himself to handle the management requirements of this position. This was not surprising, since McSly had conspired for years to make him feel inept. Just becoming aware of how this inner traitor was working in opposition to his true aspirations and his innate competence allowed Tom to change his attitudes and habits. Excited about each change and its positive payback, he continued to dig deeper in his psyche. Tom worked on taming the more subterranean levels of his personal saboteur for several years.

His efforts paid off with great rewards. Tom is now a top executive of a Fortune 500 company. He loves it, and he has proven himself to be exceptionally capable. When I last spoke with him, he was joking about how he had been such a rebel about *"dressing for the job."* Now Tom tells me that he actually enjoys the dynamics of looking great outside the office, as well.

THE CASE OF
KATHLEEN

Saboteur activity knows no gender preferences. A financially secure woman, Kathleen reported that, upon serious contemplation of her "bargain-aholic" shopping patterns, she had pinpointed a syndrome of "settling for less." She continually filled her closet (and her life) with mediocrity. This undercurrent had actually bothered her for years. Kathleen had a full wardrobe of practical, ordinary clothing, but no outfits that she really loved. Nothing she owned was of such exceptional quality and style that it made her look striking. Mulling over how she easily accepted less than her heart's desire with her clothing, she remembered other times she had let herself down. Kathleen surmised that it was her personal saboteur that had seduced her into a sexual encounter with someone she not only did not respect, but actually disliked. McSly then screamed inside her mind, *"You slut! See, you are nothing but a lowlife!"*

Exploring further, Kathleen found her McSly hard at work setting up numerous incidents in other arenas of her life, as well — incidents designed to prove her unworthy of achieving her professional and personal goals. Kathleen is a brilliant attorney in a prominent law firm on the East Coast. Needless to say, she took her McSly to court, asking for a life sentence. Currently, Kathleen has her goals well within reach and whether dressed down or up, she looks absolutely stunning.

Are you getting a picture of how a personal saboteur works? Bear in mind, McSly is a part of you, not some outside power beyond your control. At some point in your past, McSly's voice kicked in trying to protect you — like lying to your mother about how many cookies you had eaten or exactly what you were doing that mud got all over you.

Taming strategies that transform the Personal Saboteur into your strongest ally are easily incorporated into your daily life:

1. **Listen closely for the voice of McSly in your own mind and in your feelings**. Be diligent about doing so. Keep a saboteur journal, if you are the writing type.

2. **Avoid the trap of punishing yourself for not being perfect.** No one, absolutely no one, is without some faults. Self-effacing thoughts can be the sneaky doings of McSly and may result in a loss of positive, forward-moving personal power. Self-deprecation keeps you stuck.

3. **Bestow a friendly name upon your gremlin.** Reflect a sense of fun when bestowing its title.

4. **Maintain your sense of humor.** Humor contains enormous transformational energy. When you detect McSly's involvement in any event or thought, simply replay the incident in your mind, over and over, until you can laugh. Use phony laughter, if necessary; just fake it, until you make it.

5. **Repeated viewing** of your McSly incidents may also enhance your ability to make finer distinctions about your personal saboteur's habits. It is important to keep your sense of humor alive during these reviews. The rerun approach helps to remove shame and any other emotional charges. A key strategy, this process enables you to make corrections in a positive manner without degrading yourself.

6. **Clarity is the master key** that turns this villain into an energetic power that works in support of your success, rather than against you. By understanding the subtleties at work, you are free to **choose** different behavior — fully enabled to decide whether or not to allow the saboteur to have a destructive effect on you.

The ambiguity about appropriate casual workplace attire easily awakens the personal saboteur. McSly thrives on and breeds confusion. Beware of getting trapped in that mire. Later in this chapter, specific garments, accessories, and grooming that guarantee sabotage for men and women are depicted in photographs and sketches.

First, let's gain some extra mileage on McSly. Take a look at these common Workplace Warts that lead you to the Business Casual Casualties Stagnation Station.

CHOICE

When you are "at choice" with your actions and responses, you have reached a high level of freedom from the negativity induced by an active personal saboteur. Iyanla Vanzant, author of One Day My Soul Just Opened Up, *defines being "at choice" in this way:* **"Choice is the ability to recognize alternatives and possible consequences, thereby enabling the selection of that which is most desirable, admirable, and honorable. The ability to act in response to the recognized alternatives."** *– Iyanla Vanzant.*

Displaying these distasteful characteristics places you and your company at risk of being filed away into the "Going Nowhere" category — earmarking *you* as a contagious loser.

- **POISONOUS ATTITUDES** — *"No one will notice"* and *"My dress-down appearance is not important."*
- **WORN-OUT OR TIRED CLOTHING** — makes *you* look weary and haggard, with no energy or vitality. Successful people do not want to be around a deadbeat.
- **TACKY, CHEAP FABRICS** — make you look cheap. Who would want to invest in you, if you don't invest in yourself?
- **FADDISH, CUTE-SY, WHIMSICAL APPAREL** — instantly disempowers you in the workplace.
- **BAD FIT – TOO TIGHT OR OVERLY BAGGY** – Too tight can label you as preoccupied with your body or say that you come from a poverty-stricken background. Overly large can signal that you have something to hide or that you have sloppy, sloblike tendencies.
- **EXTREMELY COLORFUL ATTIRE** — Numerous colors at one time lower your professionalism, confusing the eye. The effect is clownish, or like a costume.
- **SCRUFFY FACIAL HAIR** — Mustaches and beards can put you at risk, eliciting distrust. If you have either or both, keep them immaculately trimmed and groomed. Mustaches should *never* drape far down onto the lips, unless you are an entertainer or actor and it suits your character image. Otherwise, you resemble a bandit. Ladies with facial hair or upper-lip hair — get it waxed or see an electrolysist.
- **EXCUSES OF EXTRA WEIGHT OR BUDGET CONCERNS** — Allowing these to keep you from presenting yourself in a polished, professional manner gives you "loser" status.
- **OUTDATED IMAGE** — clothing, skirt length, hairstyle, makeup. Any of these makes *you* appear freeze-framed in the past, ill-informed about what is happening in the world now.
- **FASHION ADDICTION** — Following all the latest fads, flattering or not, makes you look silly and insecure with no authentic sense of yourself.
- **PROVOCATIVE ATTIRE** — does *not* belong in the workplace. This does not mean that you turn off your sex appeal or look staid and boring. It does mean avoid these items: no low-cut tops or blouses, no pant, skirt, or top that is too tight, no too-short skirts or tops (no midriffs showing), and no see-through fabrics.
- **EXCESSIVE FRAGRANCE** — Colognes and perfumes should be used sparingly in the workplace.
- **CHEWING GUM** — Chic-less, gum chewing advertises you as a nonprofessional.
- **UNKEMPT OR FUNKY NAILS** — No one will take you seriously. All nail art is considered unprofessional. Funky colors — extremely dark or the new blue, green, or yellow shades — are not acceptable in the workplace.
- **NAKED FEET** — No socks or hosiery means you are not seriously playing the game of business, marking you as a minor leaguer, if you're in the game at all.
- **CHEAP, ILL-KEPT SHOES** — scream for bad evaluations, demoting you.

Adhere to high standards of professionalism when you are dressed down, regardless of how casually your coworkers dress. Pay close attention to your responses from others as you make positive changes. If you are teased for dressing in quality, professional casual attire, notice who is laughing. You may be hearing the snickering of someone else's saboteur. When people are uncomfortable, they often resort to teasing or put-downs to soothe their own uneasiness. Men, especially, tease each other when they are impressed rather than giving a direct compliment. Whatever tone or disguise it comes in, absorb all teasing about your upgraded image as positive feedback. Just smile and continue to wear empowering casual clothing; serious respect is around the next corner. Before long, those who harassed the loudest may start emulating you.

Career graves are casually dug by another dangerous, though subtle, manipulation of the personal saboteur: dressing solely to fit your current position. This habit boxes you in, pigeonholing you for particular jobs. Life is full of unexpected occurrences. Regardless of your position, you never know what expansion of duties or appealing opportunities might arise. **Dress down for the job you want, not for the one you have currently.**

Technology genius Ron Jenson and his wife are friends of mine. Ron, a fashion illiterate, considers clothes important only because they keep you from being naked in public (a classic engineer philosophy). One night over dinner, the subject of professional dress codes came up. Ron's company has an across-the-board casual dress code for its employees. This policy is especially lax for technical people, which is common in many computer companies. The "brains" are allowed to dress any way they please. Ron loved the flexibility of showing up for work in T-shirts, shorts, and sandals, face shaven or not.

As dinner went on, the subject turned to Ron's current technical project. He expressed frustration that, for years, he had spearheaded the design work for this new, exciting product. Now he had been told that he was *not* to be the engineer who would explain the product's technical aspects in strategic sales meetings. Ron is quite articulate, so this was puzzling. The real kicker was that a video was being made to launch the product and he had no voice in it. Instead, he had been shuffled onto another project. He had been well compensated for his brilliant work in product development, but the glory was lacking.

Ron shared how he had dreamed of discussing his pioneering efforts with this project on a technical TV talk show. I began to question him about the engineer who was to be their main spokesperson. You guessed it! That guy had been savvy enough to dress down in a professional manner, in spite of the fact that the other engineers dressed in an excessively casual manner. The marketing team could "see" this man in front of their clients, addressing the complex specifications of the new product.

Curious, I asked to interview the selected engineer. Since he was also intrigued, Ron arranged a phone meeting with Jerry. Jerry said developing computer technology was his passion, adding that he had learned early in his career about the power of a professional image. Not wanting to be stereotyped or boxed in, Jerry had fought dressing absentmindedly like the typical engineer.

I questioned Jerry about his daily dress habits at this company. He often showed up in T-shirts, shorts, and sandals, sometimes unshaven, at odd hours. However, Jerry said that he made it a point to wear nice slacks with a collared, long-sleeved shirt for staff meetings. On occasion, he would even wear a coat and tie. When he was informed ahead of time about customer meetings where his expertise was needed, he wore a sport coat.

To stay ahead of the temperamental technology game, Jerry kept a pair of khakis and a navy blazer in his work space to change into when he had to meet with unexpected VIP visitors. His theory was that even if he were wearing a T-shirt and sneakers, pressed khakis and a blazer would look acceptable, in a pinch. After speaking with him, I was still disappointed for Ron, but I clearly understood why Jerry had walked away with the prize assignment.

Are you pigeonholed? Are you allowing your personal saboteur to control how you dress for the workplace? Unchecked personal saboteur tricks create roadblocks in your career. Let's look now at specific dress-down garments and accessories for men and women, which are guaranteed to cast ugly shadows on professional reputations. There are separate sections for men and women. In addition, a unisex section depicts sabotaging habits that commonly threaten both genders.

BUSINESS CASUAL CASUALTIES (WOMEN)

As we near the twenty-first century, women in business have much to celebrate. According to a new report by the U.S. Census Bureau, one in six American businesses is now owned by women. Nevertheless, it is still a predominantly male business world.

Women must be extraordinarily careful with their choices for dress-down apparel. Females are easily disempowered by excessively casual attire in the workplace. Keep in mind that distractions diminish your personal power and jeopardize your professional effectiveness. Be shrewd when you get "down" to business.

Sleeveless Attire

You will be skinned alive with too much flesh showing. Don't be caught unarmed. Sleeves are your armor against sabotage in the business world. Sleeveless blouses, tops, or dresses *never* belong in a professional setting.

The ladies shown at right look great for a luncheon, for a date, or for shopping, but NOT for the workplace. Their overall image is not businesslike, nor does it convey professionalism. Instead, their image communicates an interest in socializing. Note that their nails are too long and too dark to add professional polish to their aura. Also, all those bracelets are sure to jingle-jangle together for a not-so-pleasing workplace distraction.

The sleeveless misconception is all too common to women who live in the warmer climates. Sleeveless or short-sleeve suits are not even manufactured for men.

FIG. 2:1 *social, **not** professional, dress*

THE ONLY EXCEPTIONS ARE THESE:

- *under a jacket*
- *as evening attire for a formal occasion*
- *at a company picnic or swim party (while participating in a business-related sports event).*

And sleeveless shirts are deemed totally unacceptable for men's business wear. This rule is no different for women who are serious about succeeding in the world of business.

T-Shirt as the Top Entree

The T stands for *T-oo* relaxed to be businesslike on its own. Solid-color, high-quality T-shirts are acceptable in most industries if worn paired with a jumper or worn with nice slacks or a skirt, topped with a jacket, vest, or sweater. Even then, T's must be pressed to command a professional status.

T-shirts worn with jeans are McSly's favorite outfit for the workplace. T-shirts teem with vitality and professionalism only when pressed and part of an attractive outfit.

Jeans, Denim Skirts, and Denim Overalls

You must be fairly slim to wear jeans in the workplace, and only then with a tailored jacket, leather shoes, and hose or socks — never with just a T-shirt. If you aspire to have your pockets lined with sweet success, denim is not the dress-down fabric of choice, even in a skirt.

Denim skirts convey a dowdy-housewife image. Extremely baggy jeans *always* illusion on extra pounds. Bag 'em for the workplace or you may find yourself singing the blues.

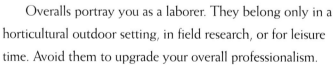

FIG. 2:2 DENIM SKIRT

Overalls portray you as a laborer. They belong only in a horticultural outdoor setting, in field research, or for leisure time. Avoid them to upgrade your overall professionalism.

Leggings with Big Sweater Tops or Sweatpants

Both examples are guaranteed dress-down sabotage in the workplace. Leggings and sweatpants carry the image of comfortable leisure or active housework — definitely not a dedicated businesswoman bound for success.

FIG. 2:3 LEGGINGS

Shorts

Shorts can shorten your career; they belong in your recreational time. The only shorts that can darken the doors of a legitimate workplace and have a professional leg up are the city shorts or walking shorts (for example, Figure 2:5). Hose are essential. Treat this garment like a pant or a skirt. The whole look must be coordinated and complete for a professional effect.

FIG. 2:4 *recreational shorts*

FIG. 2:5 *walking or city shorts*

Scruffy Shoes

Tread carefully — scuffed, nicked, dirty, sloppy, worn-out shoes will two-step you right into the Casualty Zone. The career ladder becomes even harder to climb wearing any of the shoes described above.

Scuffed toes, dented heels, and overrun soles loudly announce your destination as "Nowhere Noteworthy." The *tap-tap-tap* of a heel that has worn down to steel is a bad-rap rhythm, naming you as a loser. Maintaining your shoes should be as important as washing your hair. If not, don't expect to accomplish any major feats in your career.

Stirrup Pants or Riding Pants

Tight stirrup pants do nothing to stabilize your career. Looser stirrup pants worn with a classy ankle boot to cover up the stirrup? Only if they are high quality and if every other garment and accessory on your body is in exceptional taste, oozing with "already-made-it" success. Your overall grooming must be impeccable.

Equestrian in nature, riding pants are supposed to cling to the body like a second skin, therefore, they are unsuitable in the workplace. Why horse around with your career?

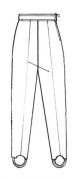

FIG. 2:6 *stirrup pants*

FIG. 2:7 *riding pants*

Short Leather Skirts

FIG. 2:8 *short leather skirt*

Hazardous no-no's. Short leather skirts, or miniskirts of any fabric, speak their own language, one not spoken in a standard workplace. Their provocative message suggests a *"let's go tango"* agenda. Overtly sexy apparel in a business setting totally erases your authority as a professional, and projects that you have no sincere commitment to your career.

Short leather skirts are sometimes acceptable in the fashion industry. To command respect there, they must be of exceptional quality and should be worn with opaque stockings.

Knee Boots with Pant Legs Inside or Thigh Boots

Unless you want to be booted out, don't wear either of these in the workplace. The look in Figure 2:9 is borrowed from the formal equestrian outfit. For riding? *Yes.* In the office? *No!* For pants to not bunch at the knees when tucked into a boot, they must fit very tightly — too tight to be appropriate for business.

FIG. 2:9 *knee boots with pant legs tucked in*

Thigh boots are for young legs only — for a hot date, worn with a miniskirt. Do *not* wear thigh boots in the office or you will find yourself knee deep in something else.

FIG. 2:10 *thigh boots*

FIG. 2:11 LARGE PRINTS

The Crayon Box or Strong, Loud Prints, and Gypsy Styles

Are you attempting to gain recognition by being a colorful person? Wearing more than three primary hues at one time makes you look costume-y, confusing and jarring the eye with distractions. Fruity prints? Neither bananas, peaches, nor cantaloupes speak a professional language.

Bold, colorful prints do make you visible (possibly unsightly) and add extra weight. They speak louder than you do, diluting your professional power. Often found in casual wear, these prints are blatantly unbusinesslike, not an advantage in the workplace. Why clown around with your success?

Gypsy looks are not mysterious in the workplace. My crystal ball says you will have a nomadic career path, always foraging.

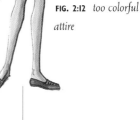

FIG. 2:12 *too colorful attire*

FIG. 2:13 SWEET PRINT

Cutesy Little Girl and Sweet Prints

All of these looks disempower women when worn for business. Expect to be treated like a child when you wear bows, barrettes, or any overtly "cute" attire. Keep your inner child alive and well; it will keep you healthy and youthful. But don't let her dress you for the office!

Wearing sweet prints, especially small floral designs, in the workplace conveys that you have little-girl attitudes or that you are uncomfortable asserting yourself in a competitive business setting.

FIG. 2:14 CUTESY ATTIRE

Floral dresses are for church, weddings, luncheons, or other social occasions; they are not appropriate for a woman serious about her career. Sweetness is a wonderful thing to have as a personal quality, but don't sabotage your business savvy by wearing these fabrics for work.

Poorly Coordinated or Incomplete Outfits

In Figure 2:16, the khaki pants and red striped blouse show no relationship to each other in color and they completely miss the mark of qualifying as a Business Casual outfit. Looking as if she hurriedly chose these garments without thinking about projecting a professional appearance, this woman conveys that she may be disorganized — especially since she did not wear a belt when her pants have obvious belt loops. Her choice of sneakers and cargo-style pants makes her appear as a factory or manufacturing worker — not the executive assistant that she is.

FIG. 2:16 *poorly coordinated outfit*

Failing to create a coordinated look with separate garments is the most common sabotaging error women make when dressing down. A good rule of thumb when combining separates is to coordinate at least two pieces in the same color family. To ensure completion of an outfit, view the entire look, asking if your ensemble could be a store display. If yes, then you are assured of a well-coordinated look.

Figure 2:17 is an excellent example of a coordinated, professional look that combines separate articles of casual clothing in differing fabrics. Even though the linen-and-cotton vest has varying colors, the

khaki-colored background coordinates beautifully with the 100 percent cotton khaki pants. With both the vest and the pant in khaki tones, she can add the contrasting white blouse (also 100 percent cotton) and still look well coordinated. The blue stripe in the vest helps to pull in the tropical-wool navy jacket — and navy and khaki are always considered a classic combination. Her well-chosen accessories add to this polished, put-together look — especially note the leather belt that is color coordinated with the all-leather shoes. And her gold earrings, necklace, and bracelet correspond with the gold-tone metal of her belt buckle. She scores high on putting together the details of this Business Casual ensemble.

Failure to Accessorize

Don't be an accessory to your own sabotage. Even the most casual outfits look more finished and polished when properly accessorized. When accessories are lacking, the nonverbal communication is that you do not pay attention to details in your work. Perhaps you have trouble completing projects?

Two common examples: 1) Your slacks, pants, or jeans have belt loops, but you wear no belt. Belt loops demand a belt! 2) Your ears are pierced, but you wear no earrings. Even if you have long hair, earlobe holes are distracting. Don't cripple your potential to reach the finish line of success.

Accessory Overload — Overly Accessorized, Rings, Multiple Earrings

Does your jewelry resemble an albatross around your neck? Overdoing accessories creates a colossal distraction, siphoning away your personal power. A woman wearing a lot of accessories at one time projects that she may have trouble making decisions, and what's more, that she may have impulsive, extravagant tendencies! If she does not use good judgment when narrowing down her accessories, how would she fare with important business matters?

To avoid accessory overload, use my "Point System" to check if you're on track or off course for a professional image. A classy, professional image does not score over 10 to 12 points for any outfit. Here's how my point system works: Count everything you are wearing as one point. Yes, everything. Give each item of clothing one point. In addition, count your shoes as one point and earrings as one. Then count your watch, or any belt, ring, bracelet, necklace, or scarf that you're wearing as one point each. All accessories (including hair ornaments) get one point each. Add up your points. If your total is over twelve, remove accessories until you're exuding professionalism and your outfit score is between 10 and 12.

A dead ringer for sabotage, heavily jeweled fingers make for a "wannabe." Wearing rings on every finger in the workplace does not encircle you with success, fame, and fortune. Rule of thumb: Never wear more than three rings (total for both hands) for a powerful, successful impact. If you have large rings or you wear an ornate watch, wear only two rings. Think "quality," not quantity.

Multiple earrings painfully limit your career options. Your ear is not a Christmas tree; you get no extra "presence" by hanging extra ornaments. If you have multiple ear piercings, wear one pair of earrings and style your hair to cover your ears to exude professional panache in the workplace. In your private time, if you want to tuck your hair back for your earrings-s-s to show, it's your biz.

Funky Nails — Nail Art, Chipped Polish, Too Long, Unprofessional Colors

Do you want to possess professional polish? Whether you are handling documents, keyboards, money, or whatever, your hands are on display and are observed more than you might imagine. Your nails automatically signal what category you're in. They can file you away as a loser or they can indicate panache and success. The biting truth is your nails are an integral part of your image.

Nail art begs not to be taken seriously and advertises that you may indulge in frivolity. "Flippant" may describe you in the workplace if you do not pay serious attention when respect is due. Rainbows, flags, polka dots, or abstracts — any artwork creates distractions, stealing power and professional influence.

Do you allow your manicure to deteriorate, chipping away at your professionalism? Chipped nail polish, broken nails, and ill-kept nails are common saboteurs for women. Ragged nails publicize that you may be lazy, disorganized, or don't care — all of which place you in the "Business Casualty Hazard Zone."

Don't wear an invisible witch's hat in the workplace. Lo-n-n-n-g, dark, hooked-like-a-hawk's-beak nails look like they belong on a sorcerer's rod slowly stirring up a murderous potion. They do not claim respect or inspire trust. Even on ordinary-length nails, offbeat colors make you look shady. Nail colors such as blue, green, yellow, purple, gold, or silver are not considered businesslike. Don't jinx your success with quirky nails.

Bunches of Bracelets or Ankle Bracelets

Charming or disarming, overdoing bracelets detracts from your effectiveness. Noisy jingling from an arm full of bangles makes for an annoying disturbance in the workplace.

Ankle bracelets tout minus-zero professionalism. They belong on the teenage dance floor, or at the beach. Like prison shackles they ask, "Who or what are you chained to?" Ankle bracelets demote you.

Mangy Hosiery

Whether sheer or opaque, snagged hose unravels your professionalism. While actual runs may not be present, little snags make your legs resemble an old screen door. (Even microfibers have a limited life span.)

Cheap, dense hosiery sold in grocery and drug stores gives a mummified look to your legs. Were you born with dead polyester skin? Quality hosiery costs more, but it gives greater returns by enhancing your overall professionalism. And usually they last longer.

Save your colored or lacy hose for the dance floor or special occasions. Don't wear them in the workplace. Colored, patterned hosiery can give your legs a diseased look. Best worn with pants or long skirts, the pattern or color can create an allure around the foot area.

UNISEX SABOTEURS IN THE WORKPLACE:

Chewing Gum

Wrap up this sticky business once and for all. Male or female, if you chew gum in a professional setting, you may as well smack your foot in your mouth too. It is impossible to show off your verbal skills with gum in your mouth. Exercising your jawline by chewing gum makes you resemble a taffy machine, and it gives you no professional pull. Instead, discreetly pop in breath mints and avoid gumming up your chance for success.

Active Sportswear

Biking shorts, tennis attire, wind suits, workout clothing, any garments in the active wear category worn in the workplace can undermine your success. (See page 12 in Chapter 1 for examples of Active Sportswear.) Regardless of how great you may look in them, they will not gain you any muscle power professionally. If you wear sport attire anyway, career advancements may not work out too well for you. Keep your goals exercised, healthy, and in top shape and you will succeed faster.

Sandals

What comes to mind when you think of sandals? Sandy beaches, vacation time, days off in the sun. Let's get down to the nitty-gritty — sandals defeat you in the game of business. Appropriate for leisure time only, sandals in the workplace communicate that you have taken unofficial time off, and you've adopted a vacation-like attitude with your job. Sandals worn with hose or socks? No, in some countries it is considered bad luck to even stand beside someone wearing sandals with socks. Not fitting in a professional environment, sandals openly invite sabotage.

Exhausted Sneakers

Thought you could sneak these by me, eh? Did McSly tell you that *"No one would notice"?* If you are wearing dirty, tattered sneakers in the workplace, your professional reputation may also be soiled. Shoes bare your unconscious attitudes — are you allowing your sneakers to air your ragged laundry?

In some industries wearing any sneaker-type shoe is not acceptable. You will not see even *new* sneakers on the feet of the major-league players in business on casual days; why do you think you can make a full-court fast break and score the winning basket with grungy, frayed sneakers?

Baseball Caps

Backward, forward, bad-hair days. Baseball caps will head you in the wrong direction for success. Unless you are working a trade show or some specific event where your company is advertising with caps, stay clear. Wearing a cap in the workplace borders on irreverence. Because they conceal your eyes, caps bill you as a poor communicator.

Eye contact is imperative for establishing and building trust. Why handicap yourself unnecessarily? Save your caps for your recreational time. Be cool and move ahead in your career. Can you pull it off?

Whimsical Attire

What are those two pigs on your T-shirt doing? Humorous apparel places you under suspicion for being involved in too much "funny business" when it is time to grant raises. Subtle touches of lightheartedness and humor (in good taste only) can occasionally be okay on dress-down days. Even then, be alert to any caution or warning signals, or the real joke will be on you.

Gals, save your parrot, pepper, and cow earrings for your time off, or you chance being a workplace parody.

Political Statements

Unless you are certain about the political persuasions of the power structure in your company, keep your personal politics to yourself while in the workplace. Wearing a political advertisement can be construed as intrusive and unprofessional — a far different statement from expressing your viewpoints when asked. Such attire is deadly for salespeople. Assuming your customers share your political stance could place you in a sad state of affairs. Vote first for your own success.

Haywire Hair or Wet Hair

Wild and woolly hair makes you appear unstable. Brilliant as Einstein? Even still, tame your haywire tresses. A good haircut is essential to portraying ultimate professionalism.

Are you allowing your personal saboteur to dampen your professional spirits? Arriving in the workplace with wet hair on casual days warrants a scathing dressing down. Torrential rains are the only exceptions. Wet tresses are grossly unbusinesslike and may hang you out to dry. If you want to be showered with success, leave your wash-and-wear hair at home.

Clothing Covered with Animal Hair

Pets are good for the soul, but not for the workplace unless you are an animal trainer or a veterinarian. For purr-fect professionalism, check all outfits for pet hair before entering the workplace. Your car seats may also be culprits if your pet accompanies you on drives. Keep a lint roller or masking tape handy in your closet and car (and use them!) so that you are not barking up the wrong tree at evaluation time.

Perfume Perils

Use perfume and colognes sparingly in the workplace. Overdone fragrance saturates you with unprofessionalism. In addition, many people are allergic to perfumes. Your scented trail may cause irritation in more ways than one.

Naked Feet

Male or female, your feet must be dressed for the workplace. No socks or hosiery may be cool for leisure time, but in the workplace this can bare your unprofessional standards. Denuding the very foundation of your business image defeats your purpose.

DRESS-DOWN CASUALTIES (MEN)

Males make up the majority of people working in business; this statistic in no way indicates that men are not easily sabotaged by wearing excessively casual attire in the workplace. Dress-down casualties involving men and their clothing choices are a common occurrence.

To be identified as a major-league player in the game of business, avoid diluting your power with the following dress-down hazards. Keep in mind that physical distractions can detract from your professionalism, jeopardizing your desired results.

T-Shirts

A T-shirt as business attire is an oxymoron. An ill-kept T-shirt really pushes the envelope. Wearing thin, low-quality T-shirts with someone else's logo advertises you as a loser in the game. They aren't even an ace when teeing off for a game of golf.

FIG. 2:18 T-SHIRT W/JEANS

At the minimum, T-shirts must be solid-colored, made of medium-weight cotton, and wrinkle-free. For business wear, they are enpowering *only* when under a jacket.

T-shirts with sport logos are simply not professional attire. Your favorite team does not belong in your workplace. Play the game of business instead.

Short-Sleeve Shirts

Short-sleeve shirts short-circuit your power, putting a chink in your armor. Don't be caught disarmed; long sleeves are far more powerful for the game of business. A man in a short-sleeve dress shirt resembles a little boy who is not ready for manly responsibilities.

A long-sleeve shirt with the sleeves rolled up commands more respect than a short-sleeve shirt. Short-sleeve knits (and sometimes silks) can be acceptable when paired with quality trousers and accessories. Even still, they communicate an attitude of leisure.

Floral, Tropical Print Shirts

These shirts communicate leisure — pool-side parties or vacations in the sun. Palm trees, coconuts, bananas, and hibiscus are not symbols for the serious businessman (unless he owns one of the Hawaiian Islands). Usually short-sleeve, these shirts are professional no-no's. They may be perfect for fun in the sun, but they're sabotage in the workplace.

Frayed, Faded Knit Shirts

Are you clinging to your knit shirts past their age of retirement? Cotton knits tend to fade and get nappy quickly. Their life

FIG. 2:20 *tropical print shirt*

span is not equal to yours. This is one of the most common saboteur tricks played upon men. Worn for casual business, tired knit shirts make you, your ideas, and your performance in the workplace look weary — saying that perhaps YOU need to be replaced.

Shirttails Out

Heads or tails? If you are betting on your shirt-tails, you are certainly not using your head. Dressing down for business in such a disheveled manner makes you a high-stakes gambler in the game. You may find your profits severely curtailed.

These two looks communicate laziness and say that you have no pride in your work. If this is your standard dress-down style, you're being tailed by your personal saboteur who will soon tuck you into the Casualty Cemetery.

Rumpled Permanent-Press Shirts and Pens in Shirt Pocket

Aha! Now that the coats have come off, your sneaky tackiness has been exposed. No press releases will be written about your important accomplishments while you're wearing unironed permanent-press shirts. Regardless of your position, wrinkled shirts announce that you have a *"get-by-with-as-little-as-I-can"* attitude about your work. Is your personal saboteur hissing how sending them out to a professional laundry would cost too much? Can you afford not to? When did you last get an impressive raise?

Pens and pencils in your shirt pocket do not make you look important. Instead the look advertises that your signature is not required on executive documents. But, oh so handy, you say? Put this in ink: Your professionalism is not linked to convenience.

Sport Coats Too Short, Shabby, and Too Tight

Are you attempting to conduct today's business with jackets from the early '80s or even the '70s? Sport coats today are a looser fit and are cut longer. I applaud you for wearing jackets; they can add authority and power. But don't risk looking like a *Has-Been* who is cloaking failure. Recycle your old jackets by passing them on to a charity.

SABOTEUR ALERT

TUMBLE-DRIED COLLARS DO NOT PLACE YOU NECK AND NECK WITH THE WINNERS IN THE RACE FOR SUCCESS.

Jeans

Not blue-chip material, denim must be immaculate and crisp to have authority in the workplace. Risky in many industries, jeans are best dressed up for dress-down days. Jeans go up in the businesslike rating when paired with long-sleeved collared shirts or with crew-neck or mock turtleneck knits.

Jeans are deadly with sloppy T-shirts. Excessively baggy jeans (you know, dropping from your waist with the top of your boxer shorts showing) may box you right into an uncomfortable corner in your career.

FIG. 2:22 JEANS W/T-SHIRT — NOT ACCEPTABLE IN THE WORKPLACE

FIG. 2:23 JEANS W/COLLARED SHIRT — ACCEPTABLE FOR DRESS-DOWN DAYS

Colorful Pants and White Pants

Playing golf? Going sailing? Brightly colored pants can look chipper on the country club golf course. In the business world, they advertise you as the clownish, zany type, someone not to be dealt with seriously. Be a colorful personality in the workplace, but leave your brightly colored pants on their hangers when dressing down for business.

White pants are leisure or nautical attire. Unless you own the big yacht waiting in port, don't be thrown overboard in the competitive waters of business.

FIG. 2:24 WALKING SHORTS ARE FOR LEISURE, NOT BUSINESS

Shorts

Are you shortsighted regarding dressing down for business? Bare legs in the workplace highlight your professional shortcomings and can make for a short-lived career.

Shorts connote leisure time; they are not protective attire for playing the game of business. Don't sell yourself short, unless you can genuinely afford to abbreviate your professional life.

Rugged Wear, Outdoor Jackets

Are you trying for *"rugged, good looks"*? You may have some tough terrain to navigate on your career path, but wearing these styles can make it rougher. (See page 13 in Chapter 1 for examples of Rugged Wear.) Unless your job has to do with the outdoors, rugged apparel is not businesslike. Save your plaid flannel shirts, hiking boots, and outerwear jackets for

FIG. 2:25 OUTDOORWEAR — NOT BUSINESS APPAREL

your recreational time, or you may find yourself professionally repelling.

FIG. 2:26 ANOTHER EXAMPLE OF OUTERWEAR

No Belt, Tired, Worn-Out Belts, Elastic Belts

Are you wasting your career efforts by going beltless on dress-down days? If you have belt loops on your pants, a belt is required. Otherwise, you may project that you ignore important details and have difficulty completing projects.

Elastic or jute (rope) belts do not convey flexibility, and they especially do not impart casual power. They speak to leisure time, and even then are sorely lacking in panache. Even with a leather front, they miss the mark of power. And don't get matchey-poo with me and say the colored stripe in the elastic coordinates with your shirt!

Tired, worn-out, roughed-up belts convey that you are not making enough money to buy a new one. Buckle up with quality leather to cinch your success.

Ties Too Short

Have you missed the point? Ties must tip the belt buckle to possess today's professional panache; anything less falls short of the mark. Ties tied too short silently say that you are *knot* currently informed and that you are *knot* successful enough to buy quality ties that tend to be longer.

If you are very tall, have a long torso, or carry extra weight around your middle, you are easily tied up by the saboteur. If you have a lengthy problem here, buy your ties at a high-caliber shop for the extra tall or big man.

Another blooper in the tie department involves wearing a dressy, high-sheen tie with a casual shirt, like a denim or chambray. Those types of casual shirts require matte-finished ties. Knit works well. In my opinion, casual ties worn with khakis or jeans do not empower the wearer. Truly empowering ties (made of 100% silk) belong with sport coats and dress trousers in the dressy-casual category.

Unpolished Shoes and Decrepit Shoes

Unpolished, ill-kept, expensive shoes forfeit the power of your influence. Unpolished, old, worn-out, or cheap shoes immediately relegate you to the "Second String." A man's shoes reveal how likely he is to succeed. What are your shoes broadcasting about you? If you cannot manage to keep your shoes in top form, what respectable career feats do you expect to pull off?

Unkempt Nails

How neat-handed are you? Regardless of your job or position, dirty, stained, jagged fingernails steal your power as an effective businessman. You will not be distinguished as an important "wheel" with unsightly nails. Men must keep their nails clipped, smooth, and clean to exteriorize complete professionalism.

Women and men must avoid extremely casual attire for business wear to minimize the risk of being a Business Casual Casualty. The saboteurs listed in this chapter are the most common, but they are not the only ones that can place you in jeopardy. Be sure to read the sections on *Empowering Business Casual Essentials* to be clear on what specific casual apparel and grooming support you in achieving greater success while enjoying the benefits of dressing down.

Bear this in mind: Consistent excessively casual dress in the workplace results in sabotage on a large scale. Don't be deceived. Often a lag time exists before the results are obvious. You may believe that you are doing fine until it is time for evaluations, raises, promotions, or renewal of contracts. Whether or not you are receiving negative feedback regarding your choices of overly casual dress, undesirable results will sooner or later catch up to you.

As the title of a book written by Dr. Andrew S. Grove, Intel Chairman, says *"Only the Paranoid Survive."*

RESULTS OF OVERLY CASUAL ATTIRE IN THE WORKPLACE

S trips you of your personal power

A dvertises you as a minor-leaguer, not seriously in the game

B etrays you — your competence, abilities, and talents

O bliterates opportunities

T hreatens your credibility and trustworthiness

A ttacks your self-esteem and confidence

G enerates distracting barriers to successful communication

E arns you less money

WHY WORK HARDER, ACCOMPLISH LESS, AND MAKE LESS MONEY?

"The apparel
oft proclaims
the man."

– Shakespeare, *Hamlet*

3

What Are You
Casually Communicating –
Before You Speak
a Word?

Clothing is a language, a coded language, a strong, silent tongue that tells all to those who listen with their eyes. As part of the human race, we all have some degree of skill for reading people. And we actively do so on a regular basis. Whether or not you are consciously aware of engaging in the process of reading the nonverbal messages from others — you do. We all do. It is not about judging someone or being critical. We are simply information gatherers. This natural function stems from the primitive part of our brain. We are attempting to know about our environment. Who is this person in our space? Is it safe? Do we need to alter our behavior to survive? Or to get what we need or want?

As human beings, we are equipped with an invisible, yet sophisticated telecommunications system. With finely attuned antennae continually on "Roam," we are broadcasting and receiving at all times. Our eyesight is a powerful component of those antennae. Accurately inter-preted or not, visual clues help us ascertain as much information about other people as possible. Initially, the most compelling visual indicators about someone are their clothing and overall grooming.

In *Looking Terrific*, Emily Chao said: **"Clothing language is an impor-tant visual code that projects our talents, our needs, our personalities, and our destination."** At this moment, go to a mirror and take an objective look at yourself. Try to see *"you"* through the eyes of a stranger. What are your clothing and grooming announcing about you? What destina-tion are you heading for? Where would your choices take you today?

Have you ever had the experience of your underwear showing or some part of your body, not intended for public display, unexpectedly revealed? Did you feel exposed? For you guys, how do you feel when your fly is *unintentionally* unzipped? Vulnerable? Naked? The truth is, male or female, **your psyche is unzipped *all* the time.** Clues to aspects of your conscious *and unconscious* thoughts and beliefs about yourself are actually hanging out there at all times. Barring any physical handicap, the ways you choose to dress, wear your hair, walk, talk, and breathe are open windows to the inner you. *You* are continually communicating something — always, whether verbally or nonverbally.

It is absolutely *impossible* to make a neutral statement. One of my clients, a prominent attorney, told me that he had lain awake at night for hours after hearing me speak on this subject at his law firm. He said that he had always taken care with how he dressed, especially for court. Yet, this theory that it was *impossible* to make a neutral statement was driving him crazy. The lawyer in him was challenged. He said his mind was obsessed with thinking of every feasible outfit that could possibly make a neutral statement. Someone dressed from head to toe in beige? No, a neutral color, but not a neutral nonverbal statement. At the mini-mum, it communicated that the person liked beige, thought they looked good in beige, belonged to a religious order that had particular tenets about beige — on and on. Frustrated, yet still driven to prove me wrong, he got up and looked up the meaning of *neutral* in the *Oxford English Dictionary*. Finding no real evidence there to support his case, he went back to bed to count sheep.

Just as he was drifting off to sleep, he had a flash of inspiration. He said it was as if he were floating on the ceiling looking down on his pajama-clad body splayed all over the bed below. (Yes, he was taking up over half the bed while leaving only a little room for his wife.) It was then that he realized it — that even when he was sleeping, his choice of pajamas or lack thereof, his body position on the bed (including legs, arms, and hands), his facial expression, and his breathing all contributed to making a (nonverbal) statement about him. Aspects of his nature and his preferences were, indeed, revealed. The next morning he called to inform me that the judge had ruled in my favor on the issue of the impossibility of making a neutral statement. His last words were that he intended to become fluent in this clothing language thing.

If while we sleep, we unconsciously broadcast information about ourselves at the nonverbal level, then when awake, we are even more actively sending signals. Statistics show that in the first thirty seconds of meeting someone, *you* determine at least three important factors concerning that person.

FIRST IMPRESSIONS
In the first thirty seconds, these three factors are evaluated (accurately or not):

- Socioeconomic Status
- Educational Level
- Desirability (to You)

Based on their appearance, clothing, grooming, posture, and expression, you size people up, usually unconsciously. What's more, depending upon your perceptions, you decide how you are going to initially respond to and interact with them. All of this in just thirty seconds? Yes, remember, it is impossible to make a neutral statement.

When you speak, your voice tones, speech patterns, grammar, and accent leave further clues about your background and lifestyle. Most people fail to recognize an important communication rule: Nonverbal messages actively transmit from a person's appearance and mannerisms while he or she is verbally communicating. Contrary to what you may believe, **what you say does not erase the impression you are making through your appearance.**

The communication model below is used widely in communication classes and by communication experts. I first encountered these statistics in my first public speaking course: *Powerful Presentations* taught by Robert Kiyosaki. This model reveals some amazing statistics about the influential role of one's physical appearance even while involved in verbal communication.

COMPONENTS OF VERBAL COMMUNICATION	
■ Words	7%
■ Tone (pitch, timbre, tempo, volume, emotion)	38%
■ **Physical/Visual**	**55% !!**

Take a look at the percentages here. All the nuances of spoken communications are listed.

Some of you probably believe that your actual words, the content of what you have to say, carry more weight than 7 percent. Do they really? Let's say that you just had a major disagreement with someone, and he or she screams at you in an angry voice with his or her face distorted and his/her fist thrust forward, *"Well, I'm sorry!"* Or, using a heavily sarcastic inflection, quietly, almost under his breath, with his jaws clenched in a tight smile: *"W-e-l-l, I'm s-o-r-ry!"* Do you feel forgiving? What if he says the same words sincerely, looking at you pleadingly, with regret dripping from each syllable, *"W-ell, I'm sor-ry."* How do you feel then? In all three instances, the words were identical, but the intended messages were entirely different.

In a professional setting, your clothing, grooming, and posture are an enormous portion of the 55 percent, representing the physical/visual in your communication. If you are exclusively invested in your content and you ignore the power of your image, you are missing a critical element of your overall effectiveness. You may be working too hard. Are you allowing a professional image to support you on a *daily* basis, especially on dress-down days?

The visual modality is a potent force in our society. You need to be concerned with not only your first impression, but also with your on-going impression. The comic strip, "Peanuts," drives this point home. In one of the cartoons, Charlie Brown notices that the fronts of Linus's shoes are freshly shined, but the backs are scuffed. Charlie Brown points this out to Linus with a question in his tone. Linus tells Charlie Brown that he knows, he shined his shoes like that on purpose. Linus said, *"I care about what people think of me when I enter a room. I don't care what they think when I leave."* While Linus was concerned with his first impression, he failed to recognize the power of his last impression.

Have you ever noticed that when someone looks marvelous, your mind does not imagine that person looking slovenly? Unfortunately, the same is true when you look lousy. **If you slob out on dress-down days, you imprint an indelible slob image of yourself in the minds of your superiors and coworkers.** If your customers or the senior executives of your company cannot easily envision you with your current dress habits performing a certain role, it is not likely that you will even come to mind for consideration when an opportunity or position comes available.

When two people of fairly equal qualifications are being considered for a job or promotion, the one who is *consistently* dressed professionally and well groomed will win every time. In my consulting work, innumerable executives have shared that they have received promotions and raises because of the constancy and reliability of their professional dress. Combined with their businesslike demeanor and attitudes, they gained the edge. Oftentimes, those individuals have been selected over and above other contenders who were better qualified in different ways.

A formal study conducted by Economists Daniel Hamermesh of the University of Texas at Austin and Jeff Biddle of Michigan State University claims that people who are *perceived* as good-looking and attractive earn considerably higher incomes than those who are not.[1] This phenomenon is not limited to occupations where looks obviously play a big part, such as acting, modeling, or sales. Their research found

A PROFESSIONAL IMAGE OPENS DOORS AND MAKES YOU MORE MONEY.

---

[1] Good Looks Can Mean a Pretty Penny on the Job; *The Wall Street Journal*, Marketplace, November 23, 1993.

that looks also account for higher earnings in jobs where appearance presumably plays no role: construction, factory work, and telemarketing. In addition, the Hamermesh-Biddle project reported that good looks may increase a worker's productivity if he or she must deal with colleagues and customers face to face, on a regular basis.

My own research coincides with their findings. An attractive professional image engenders greater confidence and higher self-esteem, which translate into better performance on the job.

Perceived attractiveness is a major component in a professional image. "Attractiveness" has definite standards in the dressed-down workplace. When determining what your professional image communicates, count your dress-down apparel as a minus. Casual dress is still relatively new to the business arena and is not *"perceived"* as professional and powerful as traditional business suits. If you want to be perceived as a serious player in the game of business and to be considered professionally attractive, you must be extremely selective with your dress-down attire. The following pages and chapters illustrate the details of *Business Casual* attire that empowers you by communicating credibility and authority, and by commanding respect.

When I use the word "attractive," I do not mean breathtaking beauty or handsomeness. Only a small percentage of the population is born with fabulous good looks, **but *anyone* can be *perceived* as attractive.** Anyone! Most people are not in touch with their most appealing qualities and features. Even if they are, they often don't know what to do with their strong points to maximize their true attractive potential. Flattering professional clothing, the right haircut, well-done makeup, excellent grooming, simple — yet rich-looking — accessories are always attractive in the workplace (and everywhere else).

Sincere joy, smiles from the heart, and positive attitudes are also always perceived as attractive. "Perceived" merely means to comprehend, to grasp mentally, or to take note of, to observe. When you perceive someone as attractive, you notice them. They are pleasant to look at, pleasing to the eye. Your eyes are literally drawn to them or to some aspect of them. There are hundreds of thousands of men and women who are far from naturally good-looking. Nonetheless, they have a polished way of dressing, carry themselves well, and exude a positive confidence. Together these qualities make them highly attractive. They are often *perceived* as striking and stunningly attractive.

With that in mind, let's look at that nebulous word, ATTRACTIVE. What is its root word? Attractiveness is simply the ability to attract, to bring in, to draw to, to magnetize what you need or want at any given time. Attractiveness is appeal. Appeal is power. Attractiveness is professionally empowering.

My mentor, Robert Pante, author of *Dressing to Win*, stresses that "**Success attracts *more* success**." He believes that if you *consistently* dress as if you were *already* successful that you will just naturally attract success (or more success) to you. Without doubt, Pante is absolutely correct. I have seen his theory proven again and again with myself, my clients, my family, and my friends.

Success leaves visual clues in one's appearance. In the movie "Pretty Woman," Julia Roberts plays a prostitute who is picked up by a wealthy businessman. She tells him that she makes $100 an hour. His response is, *"You make $100 an hour and you have a safety pin holding up your boot?"* Obviously, visual clues of her proclaimed success were absent. If she really made $100 an hour on a regular basis, she would not wear boots with a broken zipper.

Male or female, the fabric quality and condition of your clothing, your shoes, your jewelry, your hair, and your nails are all visual clues to your success level. I am not saying that you should drape yourself with status symbols. I am saying that you can never overdo real quality and excellent grooming. To nonverbally communicate success, make QUALITY your middle name.

One of my clients, *Anne*, has proven Pante's theory that a successful image attracts greater success. Anne has been my client for several years now and has undergone a major transformation of her image.

When I first met Anne, she appeared plain, looking extremely ordinary, although she was ambitious and intelligent. At that time, her mid-management position in the marketing department of a high-technology company was not making her completely happy. The promotion bug

PEOPLE PERCEIVED AS ATTRACTIVE HAVE HIGHER INCOMES
Are you maximizing your earning potential with casually attractive, professional dress in your workplace?

THE CASE OF ANNE

had bitten Anne — and it had bitten hard. She yearned to be the senior vice-president in charge of all marketing for this company. Anne told me this in confidence when we had our initial consultation. She also shared that she had a dream living deep in her heart of becoming exceptionally wealthy. Anne wanted to make a major difference in the world, and she understood that money would expand her influence. Beginning at an early age, Anne dreamed of being a philanthropist, donating huge sums of money to causes she deemed worthy, especially projects for children.

Considering Anne's goals, I recommended a complete makeover, and to her credit she did it all. She went for it, 100 percent plus. We started the process with a stylish haircut, and then we assessed every detail of her overall image. Her new haircut and highlights set off her face and silhouette in a dramatic way. Next, we updated Anne's makeup and manicured her nails. Under my direction, she gave up glasses, got contact lenses, and she had her teeth professionally bleached. Anne also bought a new watch that was a combination of sterling silver and 14-karat gold. Together, we emptied her closet of just about everything. Anne's clothing choices in the past had been unflattering to her body type, making her look heavy and frumpy, which she was not. The garments (from Anne's closet) that she donated to a charity fell far short of communicating that she aspired to be a high-powered marketing executive.

To rebuild her wardrobe, we began with new business clothes because Anne's first priority was to rise in the company. Our strategy was for her to look the part of a top executive *before* she assumed the role. Her company had a comprehensive casual dress code, and most of the employees and mid-management showed up rather sloppily. To communicate that Anne was taking her job seriously and that she was to be taken seriously, she needed a Business Casual wardrobe that was on the dressier end of casual.

Investing in herself, Anne used money from her savings to buy four striking, businesslike casual outfits, complete with shoes, hose, and earrings. We also selected these basics: two set-the-world-on-fire business suits for her important meeting days, a high-quality handbag, a soft leather briefcase. Anne wore *only* her new outfits until she could afford to add more. Each pay period she added one or two garments or accessories that allowed her to create new outfits with the other pieces. Anne bought only according to our plan, and only what looked stunning on her.

The first few weeks her cohorts teased her unmercifully about her dramatic change. More importantly, she received compliments from the CEO, other senior executives, and a few board members. In about six weeks, the VP of Marketing sent Anne to New York to represent the company in an important meeting regarding a pending contract. Was she successful? Yes — even the CEO of that company called the Vice President of Marketing (of Anne's company) just to say that Anne had done an outstanding job. He reported that they were ready to sign a contract with another company, but they were so impressed with Anne that they sealed the deal on the spot. As a result, finalizing strategic partnerships became a regular part of Anne's schedule. Within three months, she was moved up to be in charge of another division that focused on developing and managing strategic accounts. Anne continued to add to her business wardrobe as her responsibilities and her salary increased.

Eventually the Vice President of Marketing resigned. Guess who got the job? In ten short months, Anne received the hoped-for promotion to Senior Vice President of Marketing.

Anne vows that she would never have been given the opportunity to prove herself and to demonstrate her talents and skills if she had not made the change to a consistent highly professional image, even within the context of a casual dress code. She also exhibited the ability to dress in more traditional business attire when the situation called for it, and she astutely discerned when those times were. Anne claims that she would not have been sent to New York to represent the company if she had not been trusted to look the part of a professional, capable, successful person, representing a thriving, on-the-move company.

Today, Anne has built a world-class wardrobe, and she is ready to go anywhere on short notice and look fabulous. *All* of her clothing makes her look like a million dollars. She wants not a thread or a button less as she has happily reaped the rewards many times over.

There is one particular incident that I call Anne's "harvest" story. She was flying back to California from the East Coast after visiting her family for the Christmas holidays. (This incident occurred after Anne's image overhaul and her big promotion.) Anne looked chic and successful — even though comfortably casual — when she arrived at the airport that morning. When it was time to board, a flight attendant approached her, saying that a gentleman in First Class had invited her to join him there for the duration of the flight. In fact, he had already paid for her upgrade! Because she loved to fly First Class on long flights, and because she was adventurous and single, Anne accepted.

This gentleman did not turn out to be Anne's soulmate, but intrigue did occur. Anne had a marvelous time. And when they deplaned that day, Anne and the gentleman had become business partners in a technology venture that has since made them both *millions* of dollars!

Anne's dream of being exceptionally wealthy is well within reach now. She is immensely generous, giving to numerous causes. Because of her significant monetary contributions to an organization for gravely ill children, Anne was asked to be one of three national spokespersons to raise awareness and funding. Today, as the international voice for this nonprofit group, Anne has a dynamic reputation and she helps millions of children and their families. Her willingness to change and grow has paid handsomely. Waltzing with her childhood dreams, she radiates genuine happiness and confidence. Anne lives the proverb that "success attracts more success." Her results confirm its accuracy.

Anne's story demonstrates another tenet of my image mentor, Robert Pante: **"The world treats you as you treat yourself."** Anne's story embodies this statement. When she invested in herself, others were willing to invest in her. The response she received from friends, coworkers, and strangers dramatically changed when she loved herself enough to use part of her savings to invest in her dreams. The new clothing and image changes were just tools and outer symbols of how she felt about herself. They served as her "Dreamcatchers."

How do you treat yourself? What quality of dress-down clothing do you allow yourself to have and wear? I use the words "have and wear" because I have known some people who will buy nice clothing, but will not wear it regularly. They save it — the garments literally hang in their closets, seldom worn. Some of those folks even hire me to shop with them to ensure that their selections are right for them. I have even discovered some people who purchase clothing to simply hang in their closets — the price tags are never removed, the clothing is never worn. These people do not treat themselves well. They have an active personal saboteur. These folks push success away by not wearing the quality clothing they actually own.

Do you exude casual power? The best measuring stick is to look honestly at your responses from others. Are you getting the response you want from the world on a regular basis? Use the questions below as your gauge. Let's find out where you rate in treating yourself well.

This questionnaire requires your close attention to score properly. There are directions after each question that tell you how to score your answer — sometimes a Yes answer is a plus, so you add one point. Sometimes a Yes answer is a minus, so you subtract one point. The value of a Yes answer and a No answer may vary from question to question. The questions cover a wide territory so that you can gauge the overall nature of the responses you receive from others.

1. **Do you naturally attract the kind of people you want to do business with?**   *(Add 1 point for Yes; subtract 1 point for No.)*
2. **Do you naturally attract the kind of people you want as friends?** *(Add 1 point for Yes; subtract 1 point for No.)*
3. **Do you naturally attract the kind of people you want as lovers?** *(Add 1 point for Yes; subtract 1 point for No.)*
4. **Are you offered jobs or promotions in the industry or departments you desire to work in?**   *(Add 1 point for Yes; subtract 1 point for No.)*
5. **Do you get those special plum assignments?** *(Add 1 point for Yes; subtract 1 point for No.)* Every industry, every job has an occasional gem assignment. If you answered no, note the type of person who usually gets the opportunity-filled assignments.
6. **Do you receive compliments on your appearance?** *(Add 1 point for Yes; subtract 1 point for No.)*

7. Do your compliments come from people in positions you aspire to?

(Add 1 point for Yes; subtract 1 point for No.)

8. Do your compliments come from people in positions of power?

(Add 1 point for Yes; subtract 1 point for No.)

9. Do you often have to fend off people who are not your type or people who are in some way distasteful to you?

(Subtract 1 point for Yes; add 1 point for No.)

10. Do you consistently get excellent tables in restaurants?

(Add 1 point for Yes; subtract 1 point for No.)

11. Do you consistently get the worst tables in restaurants, such as near the kitchen? *(Subtract 1 point for Yes; add 1 point for No.)*

12. How do waiters treat you—are they slow to serve you?

(Subtract 1 point for Yes; add 1 point for No.)

13. Do waiters go out of their way to please you or give you excellent service? *(Add 1 point for Yes; subtract 1 point for No.)*

14. Do people tend to look away or fidget when you are speaking?

(Subtract 1 point for Yes; add 1 point for No.)

15. When you meet someone that you have only spoken with on the telephone, do they ever respond with, "You are Erin Gee? You are not at all what I expected." Has this ever happened to you?

(Subtract 1 point for Yes; add 1 point for No.)

16. Do salespeople in a crowded store find time to assist you?

(Add 1 point for Yes; subtract 1 point for No.)

17. Do salespeople in a crowded store allow others to press in, waiting on you last? *(Subtract 1 point for Yes; add 1 point for No.)*

18. Do people light up when they see you, their eyes opening wider?

(Add 1 point for Yes; subtract 1 point for No.)

19. Do people grimace when they see you, their eyes narrowing?

(Subtract 1 point for Yes; add 1 point for No.)

20. Do people step in front of you (or attempt to) when you are at the movies or grocery store? *(Subtract 1 point for Yes; add 1 point for No.)*

21. Do strangers smile spontaneously at you?

(Add 1 point for Yes; subtract 1 point for No.)

How Do YOU Rate in Positive Responses?

1 to 6 points   You are **Positive Response Disabled**, in desperate need of H-E-L-P. You are in the Danger Zone in how you treat yourself. You are invisible to most, maybe even to yourself. Are you masochistic? You think of your dreams as having no real possibility, just fantasy. You never valet park, and you are not having enough fun in life. You probably believe that casual means excessively relaxed, sloppy attire. Having no casual power, you are *total* makeover material. Could you possibly deserve and handle that much attention?

7 to 11 points   You are **Positive Response Deprived**. You are still in peril of being invisible. Generally, you are not masochistic, but you may easily slide into martyrdom. Your dreams seem farfetched, as if they would take miraculous luck to actually happen. You take pride in your practicality and like to blend in with the average. Your dress-down apparel sorely lacks any panache and is primarily permanent-press fabrics or blends of polyester. More than likely, you don't send any casual wear out for professional cleaning or pressing. With almost zero casual power, you may be the most resistant. Would you dare consider a makeover?

12 to 15 points   You are **Positive Response Deficient**. You need large doses of Positive Response Supplements, such as buying higher-quality clothing, getting regular massages, etc. You think about your dreams, but you settle for less too easily. You may have a leather interior in your car and you sometimes valet park. While you do possess some casual power, you still do not fully grasp the concept. In your dress-down clothing, you tend to cheat yourself by shopping mostly for bargains instead of going for what makes you look and feel like a million. Leap into the next level with a wow makeover!

16 to 19 points   You are **Positive Response Delighted.** You treat yourself well. Do you drive a Jaguar, Mercedes, or BMW? You valet park frequently and occasionally fly First Class. Keep striving for positive responses ALL the time, in every area of your life. I suspect you slack off in some areas — like not having only world-class casual clothing and accessories. Purge your closet of anything less and watch your casual power soar. Challenge yourself to actualize your dreams and reach your full potential. The world needs you!

20 to 21 points   You are a **Positive Response Deity**. If you scored 20 to 21 points, you always fly First Class (or do you have your own plane?). You think limousines instead of taxis. You drive the most luxurious Jaguar, Mercedes, or BMW. Your second car may be a Ferrari or a Lamborghini. You love high-quality clothing and you dress down with panache. Casual Power? Oh, yes! Life should be delicious for you. You have a lot to offer. Are you making a positive difference in the world for others? Send me your story!

How do you feel about your score? Like it or not, the responses you receive strongly indicate what you are **truly** communicating. To become more conscious of what you are projecting, start observing every tiny nuance of other people's responses to you. Some of you are screaming, *"I don't live my life for other people!"* No, of course you don't. I would not encourage you to do so. Just use other people's responses as a valuable barometer to gauge your nonverbal messages. Are you "on course" or "off course" with reaching your destination of success and greater success?

Two of my most powerful mentors, Robert Kiyosaki and Robert Pante, teach how to achieve success and experience greater joy and fulfillment in life. They go about it quite differently, each in their own style, but their end results are similar. I have combined four of their principles for my own formula for empowerment. Integrate these philosophies and become a "dream-catcher," for yourself and for others.

EMPOWERING PRINCIPLES FOR DREAM-CATCHING

"For things to change, first I must change." — Robert Kiyosaki

"The world treats you as you treat yourself." — Robert Pante

"The response you get is your true communication." — Robert Kiyosaki

"A rich, successful image attracts success and greater success." — Robert Pante

---

The nonverbal communication inherent in one's physical appearance is similar to the steering wheel of a car. For your car to go in the direction you want, you have to look and steer in that particular direction. If it is not going that way, do you get out and yell at your car, kick the tires, and blame everything but your steering? First, you have to *change* your steering choices from the inside of your car. The same theory applies here; you have to decide what your goals are, who you want to be, and where you want to go. You must consciously choose to navigate the mapped route that will take you there, including dressing the part *before* you arrive. (If you are invited to the Governor's Ball, you do not drive there first and then — and only then — begin to contemplate what clothing you are going to wear to be appropriate.)

Distractions when driving create hazards and often result in accidents with serious injuries or fatalities. This phenomenon also occurs in professional dress — a distracting, unprofessional image places your success potential in jeopardy. Are you familiar with the little voice in your head that chatters on about others' choices of clothing, haircuts, or anything that distracts you from the business at hand? Other people can experience that same voice regarding *you*.

Distractions invite intrusive static. Any aspects of your physical image that create negative distractions set up roadblocks to your communications. Remember, the physical/visual is 55 percent of verbal communication, and that figure doubles for nonverbal. Listening attentively with 100 percent focus is difficult enough without asking for interference. If you generate negative distractions, you have to work harder to have your message heard and to earn respect and credibility.

Are you dressing down to attract or to distract? Distractions can be formidable — so powerful that it is impossible to overcome them — resulting in a handicap to your personal power. When personal power is diminished, so is your likelihood of success — the best reason for professional dress standards to incorporate clean-cut grooming and simplicity of style.

When individuals or groups in my workshops name the qualities they most want to project, *power* usually heads the list. I am continually amazed at their responses when I ask them, "What is *power?*" Generally, I hear replies like, "*Control,*" "*Dominance,*" "*Money.*" I want to be perfectly clear regarding this point. When I speak of *power* in the context of "power dressing," whether power-casual or traditional business attire, I am not referring to control over another person. Dictionaries define *power* as simply **"the ability to do."** A professional image is a *power* tool because it *increases* and *strengthens* your ability to achieve.

What do *power, credibility, authority,* and *trustworthiness* actually look like as clothing, especially when you are dressed casually? Over the next few pages, revealing makeovers show how these traits can be non-verbally communicated through a casual image. These examples came

There are four main traits that are essential for you to project in order to perform well in any industry.

PERSONAL POWER
CREDIBILITY
AUTHORITY
TRUSTWORTHINESS

These qualities, when authentically communicated, always boost your ability to succeed.

directly from my client files. The artist copied real-life photographs of the transitions, the before and after. At times, hair color or another feature was changed to disguise the identity of the individual. Be sure to read the commentary of the "Before and After" shots to catch the finer distinctions of precisely which garments, grooming, accessories, and postures communicate these qualities.

INSPIRING TRUST:

Before, Jim does little to inspire trust. His shaggy hair and beard narrow his eyes, giving his face a closed, menacing look. His shabby knit shirt, brown jeans, and frayed sneakers announce loudly that he is sorely unsuccessful as an accountant. Jim's posture, especially his slumped shoulders, apologizes for his presence. He appears negative, depressed, and closed, especially with his hands in his pockets. Jim's accounting firm supports a casual dress code. Even so, would you be excited about hiring him to handle your taxes and financial accounts, based on his appearance in Figure 3:1? If you answered yes, let's hope that your affairs are not too complex because his nonverbal communication suggests that Jim suffers from an acute lack of attention to detail, at least in his professional presentation, especially his attire.

Do you recognize Jim as the same man *after* his makeover? Would you be inclined to trust him? Jim courageously shaved his ten-year-old beard and moustache after learning that facial hair could unconsciously elicit distrust from others. Initially, he had grown it to make him look older and more intelligent — or so he thought. Actually, because he was concerned about his receding hairline, Jim had relished his ability to grow facial hair. (In fact, Jim actually had a lot of hair. He had overreacted to a slight thinning of hair on the sides of his forehead.) Over the years, he had allowed his beard to get scruffy to the point where it was distracting and dragging him down.

The shave and haircut transported Jim into living in the current world. The starched-collared blue shirt and navy jacket elevate his visual presentation, increasing his personal power immediately. Dark

FIG. 3:1 *Jim "before" makeover*

blue is an excellent color to inspire trust on an unconscious level, as are clean-cut grooming and crisp clothing. To project ultimate trustworthiness, Jim should not have his hands in his pockets. When inspiring trust, your hands should be easily seen to communicate that you have nothing to hide and to invite conversation from others. While Jim was excited about his makeover, he was feeling a bit shy about his face showing so clearly (and being photographed) after years of hiding behind a beard. Jim was surprised that he had to fight the urge to put his hands into his pockets.

We finished Jim's professional, yet dressed-down look with high-quality wool trousers, a leather belt, and leather hard-soled shoes. Jim now looks as if he handles lucrative accounts. Visually inspiring trust and credibility, Jim exudes casual power.

One year after Jim's makeover, he landed a job with one of the big eight accounting firms. He reported that his makeover got him excited about his life again; through this process, Jim reconnected with his hope to achieve his dreams.

FIG. 3:2 *Jim "after" makeover*

INSPIRING TRUST:

Paula is a commercial real-estate agent. One of the partners of the company hired me to work with her. Paula's job was on the line if she did not change to a more professional look.

The Before Paula: Her frizzy, wiry hair contributes to a look of instability in her overall image. The gypsy-like dress adds to her doubtful appearance, doing nothing to inspire professional trust. Paula has been an active agent in the same city for seven years. Would you have guessed? She has struggled financially and, not surprisingly, has failed at landing long-term corporate management accounts. Paula claims that she thought that the '90s dress-down trend made the theories of professional dress obsolete —

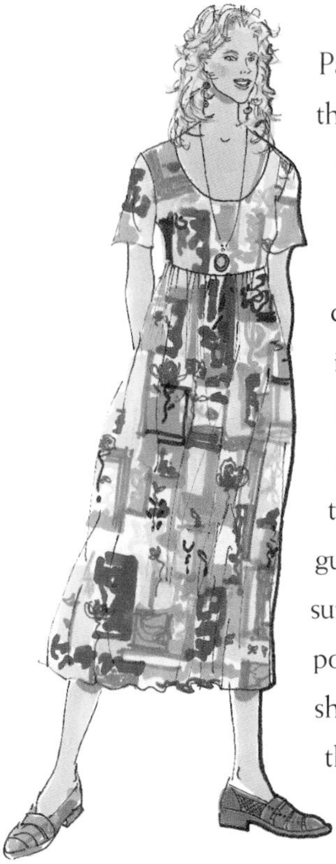

FIG. 3:3 *Paula "before" makeover*

FIG. 3:4 *Paula "after" makeover*

especially in real estate. She has learned differently as her income has dramatically increased since her makeover.

Smoothing out Paula's naturally curly hair was not enough. She needed another cut and color to give her a capable, trustworthy look upon first impression. The shorter cut made her wavy hair easier to manage as well as highlighting her strong jawline. Paula had been using an inexpensive home color-bleaching kit on her hair — and it showed. We decided to go back to her natural color, a lovely light auburn that enhanced her beautiful soft, brown eyes and her skin tone.

We chucked the multicolored, overly casual dress, but Paula strongly stated that she is most comfortable in long flowing lines. Her new chocolate-brown skirt is long and still has some fullness, but the overall look is simply tailored. The multicolored tweed jacket satisfies her urge for color, but it exudes professionalism. Since Paula is 5' 4" tall, we chose a solid-colored brown top to go under the tweed jacket. Worn with the brown skirt, this gives her one line of color all the way up, including the brown boots. The tweed jacket works as a dynamic accent; this makes her look taller and creates a more pulled-together vertical image. Simplicity and high-quality fabrics work together to inspire trust.

Instead of the distracting, long-feather-dangle earrings in Figure 3:3, Paula now wears an unusual amber earring that picks up the detail from the button on the jacket. This congruency adds an air of polish and trustworthiness. High-quality suede boots and a soft briefcase add to Paula's professionalism. Are you inspired to trust her capabilities now?

Paula jumped on the professional dress bandwagon and has remained consistent with the goals of her makeover — she always puts her best foot forward. Four years after Paula's makeover, where is she? Paula is a full partner in the commercial real-estate firm where she began as a struggling agent. Paula's current reputation as a dynamic businesswoman precedes her and opens doors automatically.

DRESS-DOWN CHARACTERISTICS THAT INSPIRE TRUST

IMPECCABLE GROOMING

- Clean, shiny hair, professionally cut (Hair can have flair, but not too outrageous in style or color)
- No facial hair
- Squeaky-clean body (Not too much perfume or fragrance, especially true for men)
- Well-kept nails, clean and manicured

PRISTINE CLOTHING AND ACCESSORIES

- Clothing must be spotless, pressed, and well-tailored

  Pants and trousers, regardless of fabric, should have crisp creases
- Good quality fabrics — simple, tailored lines best
- Harmonious blend of colors and textures of fabrics
- Blue tones* — navy blue, dark blue, and royal blue positively affect the perception of trust according to color psychology experts

  *Men wearing brown suits tend to elicit distrust. This is not true for women.
- High-quality, well-maintained shoes
- Simple high-quality jewelry

  Women — metal watches; not too many accessories worn at one time

  Men — metal watches; no neck chains

FRIENDLY, POSITIVE DEMEANOR

- Eye contact — establish and maintain
- Erect posture — shoulders back
- Open body language — trustworthiness has nothing to hide

EXUDING PERSONAL POWER:

True personal power comes from within. It can be enhanced and developed, but it cannot be given. However, I find that most people are not in touch with their innate power. Often, with the right haircut and empowering clothing, their body shifts and a sense of power just pops out. It is easily observed by others. For example:

REAL TRUST IS EARNED.

These dress-down characteristics help you gain the opportunity to demonstrate your trustworthiness. Dress the part to inspire trust, then win further trust.

Rebecca is an attorney. She graduated from law school six years ago, but she failed to graduate her girlish collegiate look. The senior partner of her law firm, also a woman, asked Rebecca to upgrade her image. The firm was rapidly growing, and she needed to introduce Rebecca to new clients — all wealthy. She wanted them to feel confident about Rebecca's ability to handle the legal entanglements of their estates. Rarely involved in litigation, the firm had a semicasual dress code. Of course, with court appearances, traditional suiting was expected. Rebecca's work was excellent; it was only the professional image that was lacking.

First, we gave Rebecca a new hair style. Getting rid of the sweet-little-girl hairdo, including barrettes, gave her a sophisticated look instantly. Her makeup needed fine-tuning to brighten her pretty face and to accent the strength of her jawline. The long floral skirts and soft-shirt jackets of her college days had to go. To bring her up to date, we dressed her in a high-quality, businesslike pantsuit. The jacket, exquisitely tailored, adds a sense of potency to Rebecca's image. Her I'm-just-a-girl flats were traded in for low-heeled classic pumps that exude high-dollar class. Even though dressed down from conventional lawyer garb, Rebecca exudes personal power and commands respect.

Rebecca's makeover took place a few years ago. Ambitious by nature, she is the personality type that takes action when she gets information that can help her succeed. When Rebecca assimilated how a professional image — when paired with her intelligence and her credentials — could take her to the top, she went for it wholeheartedly. Rebecca's success story is similar to Anne's (found earlier in this chapter). After upgrading her image, Rebecca's success soared. She was made a partner in the law firm in only one year, a time frame that broke all precedents for that firm. She now owns a beautiful home — one that by most standards would be called a mansion — and she has her own driver to transport her through the large city she inhabits. Rebecca is happily married to a successful architect, and she is living the good life!

FIG. 3:6 *Rebecca "after"*
makeover

EXUDING PERSONAL POWER:

John is a stockbroker. His prestigious firm has two casual days a week. John was mystified about dressing down in anything other than khakis and golf shirts, with sneakers or soft-soled deck shoes. He had no power-casual clothing in his closet, nor did he grasp the concept. Being small in stature, John felt that he worked overtime to establish a powerful, notable presence, especially when dressed down. Before his makeover, John looks ordinary.

The power-casual outfit you see John wearing in Figure 3:8 is one of the many he purchased during our shopping expedition. Once he experienced himself in my definition of power-casual attire, he was hooked. With John's dark coloring, we chose black as his best neutral color to build a wardrobe around. The triple-pleated slacks are of exceptional quality, 100 percent refined, tropical wool; the excellent drape of the fabric proclaims superb quality. Dark slacks combined with a black-and-beige herringbone jacket brings the black color up the body but adds light toward his face. This makes John look taller. He still gets to wear a soft knit shirt, but it is one of exceptional fabric quality. The lizard slip-on shoes and tipped belt finish his power-casual look, adding richness and panache. While John works in his office, the jacket can stay on the back of his chair, if he likes.

We updated John's haircut by getting rid of the left-sided part he had coaxed for years. We had him switch to a metal watch, which added manly strength to his overall image. Looking this successful, John can go anywhere in the world dressed down, and still exude personal power and command respect.

Six months after John's makeover, he got a substantial raise and he met the woman of his dreams — a classy lady. John says that she would never have looked twice at the "Before" John. Today, they are happily married and John's stock portfolio continues to go up in value.

FIG. 3:7 *John "before" makeover*

FIG. 3:8 *John "after" makeover*

Remember, power means "the ability to do." Inherent in possessing power is having choices. Fine clothing communicates that the wearer has unlimited options, not constrained by budget concerns. Poor clothing communicates the opposite. As in a negotiation, personal power drops if one "needs" the deal so badly that there is no choice but to consent to unfair demands.

To nonverbally communicate power, looking successful and choosy is part of the package, and so is wearing current, but not trendy, classic clothing. Outdated clothing says that you have not made enough money to have the option of purchasing clothes recently.

DRESS-DOWN BASICS THAT COMMUNICATE POWER

HIGH-QUALITY CLOTHING AND ACCESSORIES

- Rich, dark colors

  Black and navy are the best power neutral colors. Dark, rich shades of green, red, brown, and taupe also project a sense of power.

- Quality natural-fiber fabrics
- Harmonious color schemes — tone on tone, monochromatic dressing, or coordinated separates
- Long sleeves — a must to communicate maximum power
- Straight-lined tailored garments
- Excellent-quality shoes and belts, maintained perfectly
- Simple, expensive-looking jewelry (metal watches only)
- Shoulder pads, small — important for women
- Jackets and sport coats always add distinction and power — must be of quality fabric and a superb fit

IMPECCABLE GROOMING

(See grooming list on how to inspire trust, page 73)

POSITIVE DEMEANOR   (See demeanor list on how to inspire trust, page 73)

- Firm handshake
- Confident attitude

  Personal power resides in your confidence to open doors and access other options. (Real power does not boast or throw weight around unnecessarily.)

COMMUNICATING AUTHORITY:

Lawrence is an upper-level manager in a high-tech company that has an across-the-board casual dress code. He aspires to be the CEO of a computer software company that does international business. To accomplish this, Lawrence must increase the authority he nonverbally communicates. An outdoors kind of guy, Lawrence is accustomed to dressing in an overly relaxed manner — too far down the casual ladder to project that he is capable of becoming an authority figure.

Authority always speaks and dresses with hints of formality. In his plaid shirt, faded jeans, and hiking boots, Lawrence completely fails to project any indication of formality. He doesn't even appear to be upper-executive material. He falls even shorter of looking like the CEO of an international company.

Lawrence eagerly cooperated in his makeover, and it shows. He thought the military look made him appear authoritative, but his hair was too short for his large head. Instead of looking authoritative, he looked more like he was recovering from chemotherapy. We had to let his hair grow a few weeks for the short and classic — yet vibrant and healthy — style of Figure 3:10.

FIG. 3:9 *Lawrence "before" makeover*

Communicating authority incorporates many of the characteristics from inspiring trust and exuding power. We dressed Lawrence in current classic (not faddish) clothing, which is especially important to exude an aura of authority. In Figure 3:10, he is wearing a high-quality, tropical-wool suit in black, which he found amazingly comfortable. Paired with the dark suit, the crisp-white, long-sleeved, fine-cotton banded-collar shirt exudes formality, yet is dressed down from the traditional suit-and-tie look. The shirt was not heavily starched, but the collar and cuffs were impeccably pressed. Contrasting color tones —

FIG. 3:10 *Lawrence "after" makeover*

dark with light — lend a definite air of authority. High-quality, all-leather tie shoes (not slip-ons) and a high-caliber, all-leather dress belt add the finishing authoritative touches.

Lawrence was shocked at how comfortable his new duds felt on his body. His powerful, commanding reflection in the mirror wowed even him. When I last spoke to Lawrence, he had received two job offers — both for CEO positions.

COMMUNICATING AUTHORITY:

Susan is an art history professor at a major university, and she is up for tenure next year. Intelligent? Most definitely, yet Susan has a tentative look that does not bode well for her goals. Her physical presence lacks authority and power in Figure 3:11, before her makeover. Susan's stringy hair must be cut, otherwise she will look like one of her students or a struggling artist. Her pale face with no makeup and her baggy clothing add to her lost waif image.

Would you recognize Susan as the same woman now? We layered her baby-fine hair so it did not hang limply around her face. Minimal makeup adds life and vibrancy to her delicate features. We dressed Susan in a steel-blue ensemble with a crisp, white vest blouse. The contrast of white with dark tones silently speaks with authority. The steel-blue fabric matches her eye color, bringing Susan's "knowing" eyes out from hiding. Classic suede pumps (closed toe and heel) with pewter-toned jewelry complete Susan's professional look. Would you now believe that she is an international authority on art history?

Susan reports that she no longer doubts her own skills. After her makeover, she pursued and won a leadership position on a national committee, claiming that she is now comfortable asserting herself as the authority figure she truly is.

FIG. 3:11 *Susan "before" makeover*

FIG. 3:12 *Susan "after" makeover*

DRESS-DOWN BASICS THAT COMMUNICATE AUTHORITY

FORMAL, BUT CASUAL

Authority always requires a certian formality, especially when dressed down.

- Dark colors, often mixed with white or a light hue for a strong contrast. Black and white is considered the most authoritative combination by color psychology experts. The uniforms or robes of authority figures such as clergymen, judges, nuns, and law enforcement officers are usually solid black or midnight navy, sometimes mixed with white. Business power suits are typically dark worn with a white shirt or blouse. Black-and-white contrast around the face does not suit everyone's natural coloring. In that case, use black with ecru, or stick with monochromatic dark colors. You can also create a strong contrast with other dark tones, like black and red, black/brown, etc.
- Long sleeves — a must to communicate maximum power
- Simple, classic garments
- Quality fabrics (does not mean designer labels)
- Shoes — high-quality and immaculate

  Men: All-leather tie shoes are best. Can have a *dressy* slip-on, if polished and in top condition.

  Women: Closed toes and heels (no higher than 3")

  Classic Pumps are the most authoritative (does not mean a plain boring shoe that has no style)

  No flats

IMPECCABLE GROOMING — See Trust list, page 73.

POSITIVE DEMEANOR — See Trust and Power lists, page 73 and 76.

- Listens well, uses words judiciously, and does not talk incessantly or at inappropriate times. (Do not mistake this attitude for aloofness.)
- Revere others' opinions, and respect yourself and your own abilities to command homage from those in positions of authority.

CONVEYING CREDIBILITY:

Credibility is closely linked with trustworthiness, but there is another aspect to its meaning I want to focus on. To succeed in any field, an image that is credible or congruent with what you do is important. This does not mean that you become pigeonholed in a certain position, but you communicate through your image that you are believable for the business you are in.

FIG. 3:13 *Claudia "before" makeover*

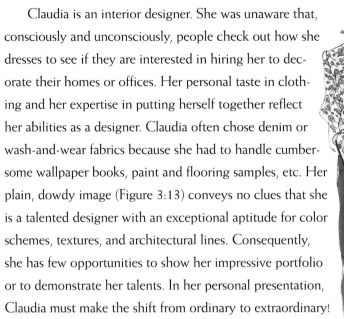

Claudia is an interior designer. She was unaware that, consciously and unconsciously, people check out how she dresses to see if they are interested in hiring her to decorate their homes or offices. Her personal taste in clothing and her expertise in putting herself together reflect her abilities as a designer. Claudia often chose denim or wash-and-wear fabrics because she had to handle cumbersome wallpaper books, paint and flooring samples, etc. Her plain, dowdy image (Figure 3:13) conveys no clues that she is a talented designer with an exceptional aptitude for color schemes, textures, and architectural lines. Consequently, she has few opportunities to show her impressive portfolio or to demonstrate her talents. In her personal presentation, Claudia must make the shift from ordinary to extraordinary!

FIG. 3:14 *Claudia "after" makeover*

For credibility, Claudia needs to embody the same sophisticated flair that she can bestow upon a room. To generate interest through her appearance, she should strive to look striking, on a daily basis. Note the example in Figure 3:14. While Claudia's jacket is still a floral, it has rich pizzazz. The silk jacquard fabric with red, olive, and brown highlights adds an exquisite quality to the classic one-button jacket. Olive/brown pants coordinate beautifully with the jacket, as does the brick-red silk blouse. The entire ensemble is in superb taste. She has attended to every detail with her jewelry, hosiery, and shoes. Her overall image is now intriguing and demonstrates her extraordinary capabilities as a designer.

Soon after Claudia's makeover, another designer (who was too ill to work) referred her to a doctors group that was redecorating their offices. While going down in the elevator after that appointment — with chic bag of fabric samples in hand — two attorneys asked her to take a look at the suite of offices that they were planning to remodel. They were so impressed with her professionalism and her design work that they introduced her to their friend, a well-established architect. Claudia has been exceptionally busy from referral business ever since and is now looking for a second assistant.

Conveying Credibility:

Ben is in sales. He and his wife run their own business. They are affiliated with one of the largest network marketing companies in the world. The company is structured on a multilevel marketing plan. Ben is working on building a profitable downline and he has only been mildly successful. He claims that a major portion of his business involves networking on the golf course. Ben often wears golf clothing to call on prospective clients. What's more, his choices of golf outfits reveal his poor taste. Ben is color-blind, which also complicates his ability to put together coordinated outfits. (Before his makeover, he had no system in his closet to help him identify certain color tones.) When calling on prospects, he has begun to hear comments about how he squeezes in appointments between golf games. People had begun to ask just how long he had been in this business, implying that they question his credibility.

Ben shared with me that he wants to create a relaxed atmosphere to put other people at ease. He thought he was projecting a casual image that said that he did not have to work for someone else. Ben was naive; his overall nonverbal communication actually said that he lacked success, ambition, and professionalism. He was unaware that he was sending the message that he did not take his business seriously. To succeed, Ben must look trustworthy, intelligent, and approachable, but most importantly, he must look like an accomplished winner to get others excited about joining his team.

Ben needed an image that portrayed him as the conscientious, savvy, ambitious guy he is. In Figure 3:16, the olive brown trousers powerfully complement Ben's blond coloring. The rich fabric of his light tan shirt silently says he knows money and its benefits. The micro-check sport coat, in brown/black/olive, adds power and an air of authority to his dressed-down image.

FIG. 3:16 *Ben "after"*
makeover

Impeccable grooming, high-quality lizard slip-on shoes and belt, and a 14-karat gold watch (subtle but rich, no flashy diamonds) contribute to the impact of Ben's overall credibility.

Within a few short weeks of his makeover, Ben tripled his downline. One of the couples he enrolled is a real go-getter type. The man is a pediatrician, and his wife is a CPA. They helped take Ben to a greater level of success because they instantly put in place a dynamic downline. Ben shared with me his excitement and told me that he knew that before his makeover, he could not have attracted that particular couple. They would never have listened to what he had to say unless he was projecting that he had something they wanted a piece of. Ben's wife also went through the makeover process, and today as a couple, they are a powerful force helping many others enjoy the benefits of abundance.

DRESS-DOWN BASICS THAT CONVEY CREDIBILITY

KNOW YOUR INDUSTRY

Analyze the details of your business to learn what qualities are most needed to project credibility in your field.

- Finance — a classic image (in excellent taste)
- Advertising, art, or beauty industry — flair and glamour (in good taste)
- Sales — a professional, successful image that inspires trust. Sell yourself! (Regardless of what you do, you have to sell yourself or your ideas, if not a service or product.)

DRESS-DOWN ON THE DRESSIER SIDE OF CASUAL

- A slipshod image only gives you credibility as a slob
- Read carefully the Clothing and Accessories tips from the *Inspiring Trust* list, page 73

IMPECCABLE GROOMING

- See *Inspiring Trust* list for Grooming, page 73, and the *Communicating Personal Power* list, page 76

POSITIVE DEMEANOR

- Be authentic, honest, sincere
- See *Inspiring Trust* list for Demeanor, page 73
- See *Communicating Personal Power* list for Demeanor, page 76

By using these tips, you are more likely to be offered chances to perform, whether or not you are deserving. Nonetheless, after the first impression, the task of proving that you are believable and trustworthy awaits you. The same holds true for exuding personal power and communicating authority.

On the other hand, if you truly possess these qualities but are not dressing that way, you are working too hard and may not be getting the breaks you deserve. Tap the power of your image as a business leverage.

"*A man cannot dress, but his ideas get clothed at the same time,*" wrote Laurence Sterne in *Tristram Shandy*. Take his words to heart to avoid being a casual casualty when dressing down for business. Remember, you are *always, always* conveying nonverbal messages. Employ the nonverbal realm to work on your team — FOR you, rather than against you. Listen and observe closely the silent language that broadcasts your and others' real communications.

Life has aspects over which we human beings have no control. That's even more reason to take charge of what we can. Your image is one thing you control completely — you actually have a monopoly on it.

Right now — today — take control of what you are casually communicating, *before* you speak a word.

"You can have
whatever you want,
if you
dress for it."

— Edith Head

4

Get Ahead —
Be Casually Smart
in the Workplace

Do you want respect, recognition, a raise, a promotion? Then dress for the position you want before you have it, particularly when dressing down. Essential to getting ahead in your profession, this concept must never be ignored.

The nonverbal communication inherent in your consistent appearance has proven its significance as a tool that gives you the edge. My files bulge with testimonials from business professionals, relaying how their businesslike image propelled them upward to promotions, raises, and new opportunities. Many share that often they were competing with others more qualified or more experienced than they. Yet because of their polished style of dress — even when casual — they were perceived as more professional and more astute.

Autosuggestion plays a star role in the results of an empowering business image. Nonverbal interplay works in two ways. It sends signals to others about you, and it sends messages to your subconscious mind about you.

When you send signals to others (and you always do), it affects their response to you. When the messages go to your subconscious mind, it affects your attitudes about yourself. Unconsciously, this impacts your demeanor. Your demeanor reflects your deeper beliefs about yourself by the way you hold your body, carry yourself, breathe, walk, talk, and behave, in general. Autosuggestion influences your attitudes about yourself, affecting your overall demeanor, which affects how others respond to you.

**NONVERBAL COMMU-
NICATION WORKS ON
TWO MAJOR LEVELS:**

*1) It sends signals to others
about you.*

*2) It sends messages to **your**
subconscious mind about
you.*

ARRAYING YOUR MIND — WIN THE MENTAL GAME:

Being well dressed and casual is NOT an oxymoron. The dress-down clothing you choose to wear also transmits powerful suggestions to others *and* to your psyche. The famous architect, Frank Lloyd Wright, a master of aesthetic form as demonstrated by his beautiful, well-renowned buildings found throughout the world, had some profound words regarding clothing:

> **"We all know the feeling we have when we are well dressed
> and we enjoy the consciousness that results from it. It
> affects our conduct. I have always believed in being careful
> about my clothes, getting supremely well dressed, because
> I could then forget about them."**

Go back now and reread this quote. Again — and again. This says it all. When my clients fully understand, embody, and daily live this quote, I graduate them with a Ph.D. in the School of Dress and the Academy of Being True to Self.

Next, let's take an in-depth look at Wright's insightful words by dividing his statement into two parts. The first segment states, *"We all know the **feeling** we have when we are well dressed and we enjoy the **consciousness** that results from it. **It affects our conduct.**"* This addresses the *feeling* of being well dressed and its relationship to our behavior. Ordinarily, most of us have some memory that allows us to access this feeling Wright described. Unfortunately, for most of us, these memories revolve around formal occasions exclusively.

Take a few moments now and reconnect with some incident in your life where *you* felt you were magnificently dressed. It can be any time; the key is that you *felt magnificently dressed*. When you have fully reconnected with your memory, take a deeper look.

- How did you feel overall?
- Did you feel beautiful, handsome, powerful?
- Were you full of energy, as if you could do or achieve anything?
- Could you more readily see the beauty in your environment and in others?
- How did other people respond to you? Were they complimentary, attentive, and eager to please you?
- Did you behave, respond, and think in a different manner from your usual?

Why leave these feelings in some memory? Dress to have these experiences with regularity in your everyday life.

Chic, casual images strike a profile for success. To leap ahead in your career, intentionally dress supremely — though informally — when dressing down for business. Being well dressed opens doors, especially important doors, and sets the tone and stage for success to occur. From there, the *quality* of your performance far outweighs your appearance. Frequently misunderstood, however, is the concept of how the way in which you physically present yourself *can be* indelibly linked to your performance.

Theater has used the concept of character dressing to bring forth more authentic performances from actors for centuries. All cultures, dating back to primitive times, have used masks and costumes to help achieve altered states of consciousness. Our current society employs uniforms and other costumes designed to evoke a respect of authority: Policemen's uniforms, nuns' habits, judges' robes, and clerical collars all command a fundamental regard from almost everyone. These types of jobs have an implied code of ethics that accompanies their uniforms.

The uniform becomes a representation of the implied code of ethics, so it also affects the wearer's psyche. Business clothing, whether you are dressing up or down, is no different.

Wright claims that being well dressed affects one's conduct. My findings take his claim further: **We act in accordance with how we are dressed.** It is human nature to take ourselves and our tasks more seriously when we are well dressed. My friends sent their son to a private high school this past year. He was reluctant to attend because he had to wear a uniform, a mandatory coat and tie. He made the change, kicking and screaming all the way. After several months, he unexpectedly announced, *"You know, I think better when I am dressed well for school. My mind just works better."* Of course, his parents applauded this admission (as they fell off their chairs in astonishment).

Professional clothing can be *your* "costume" that gives you the edge, enabling *you* to perform with excellence on the stage of business. Have you ever been to a costume party and found yourself behaving differently? Just the act of putting on certain attire can change your behavior. Use casual clothing to your advantage. Allow it to affect your conduct and positively influence you when you dress down for the office.

Wright said that he enjoyed the consciousness that resulted from his being well dressed. What exactly is our "consciousness"? Webster's Dictionary defines consciousness as *"the totality of one's thoughts, feelings, and impressions."* Notice that your impressions — your perceptions — are included with feelings and thoughts in the totality of conscious awareness.

Psychological studies have shown that feeling (emotion) often follows thought. For example, right now if I were to start focusing my thoughts upon my Dad's death several years ago, I would immediately begin to feel sadness. If I continued those thoughts, tears would start flowing and I would become even sadder. At times, emotions can have an independent life from thought, seemingly arising out of nowhere. However, I have experienced that my emotional state usually corresponds directly to whatever subject I am thinking about. First, I have a thought about something, then an emotion arises in response to the thought. Whatever I am thinking and feeling, at any given time, affects my perception of myself, of others, and of my environment. The Buddha said it well: *"We are what we think. All that we are arises with our thoughts. With our thoughts, we make our world."*

Have you noticed that when you are feeling happy, positive thoughts actually occupy more of your mind? During those times does the world look different to you, perhaps alive with more sparkle and beauty? Do people seem friendlier, nicer, and more accommodating? Conversely, if you are feeling down or depressed, have you ever observed how negative your thoughts and memories become? And how it is easier to see the ugliness in yourself and the world?

Dressing too casually for the workplace allows negative thoughts and feelings a louder voice in your psyche, your consciousness. In turn, that throws one's performance into a negative spiral. On the other hand, dressing well, especially when casual, renders greater confidence by triggering empowering thought patterns that you're capable of handling whatever the task may be. Your willingness to extend yourself in a confident manner to others influences their impressions of your abilities in a positive way.

The second half of Wright's statement may address some of your fears. **"I have always believed in being very careful about my clothing, getting supremely well dressed, because I then could forget about them."** Are some of you hearing mind chatter, psychobabble, about becoming a clotheshorse, obsessed about fashion? In fact, the opposite is true. When you can walk out the door and KNOW that you are "supremely well dressed," whether dressed down or dressed up, you can then forget totally about how you look — *for the entire day*. Then you can go **full power** into the situation or task at hand with much greater confidence and vitality. By full power, I mean completely focused in present time, with increased wattage, voltage, and *ability* at your command.

McSly's voice saps your valuable energy. Any doubt, conflict, or compromise about your clothing or appearance — conscious or unconscious — takes energy to deal with. Preoccupying distractions are fatiguing on a mental, emotional, and physical level. When this dynamic is arrested, you literally have more mind power available to you. Being appropriately well dressed silences your inner dialogue. What's more, the other person's psychobabble about you is diminished

or it is channeled into interest. Consequently, other people are freer to interact with you, giving you their full attention.

Generating positive interest just by the way you present yourself — *before* you say even one word — is a plus in business. Knowing yourself, what you are about, is the primary cornerstone to creating your own interesting look. An integral aspect of knowing what you are about is being in touch with what you want to achieve. Decide on three long-range goals for yourself and post them inside your closet door or somewhere visible to you when you are getting dressed. Make a point to review them on casual days.

Demonstrating dress-down chic captures the interest of the powers that be in your industry, giving you that all-important edge. As we have said earlier, anyone can look more powerful and professional in a quality suit, but looking powerful and professional in casual wear turns heads in today's arena of business. If you aspire to rise in your company or any other, if you aim to make more money, if you desire to be recognized, then *always* look exceptionally professional in your workplace. Staying on the dressier side of casual wear facilitates achieving those kinds of goals. Yes, be you, claim your own uniqueness, but *always, always, always* look professional.

While it is important to fully claim your individual uniqueness, your race and your ethnic or regional background have nothing to do with your professional look for the workplace. Oprah Winfrey, television's most successful talk show host, does not dress in African attire, even though she is African American. This in no way reflects her attitudes about her roots. Dr. Deepak Chopra, renowned author, does not wear Indian clothing or accessories when filming his videos or making public appearances. Both Oprah and Dr. Chopra are immensely respected and have great followings. Their sphere of influence is gigantic. If they had chosen to consistently dress to reflect their heritage, they would have limited and pigeonholed their public identities. If you choose to make a statement about your heritage in the way you daily present yourself, you will have to work harder to be taken seriously as a business person, regardless of your occupation.

As a native Texan, I can safely say to the men from the Southwest who wear cowboy boots with their business suits that the same concept applies. Unless your business is agriculture or country-western entertainment — neither of which requires suits on a daily basis — cowboy boots immediately box you into a region and a particular mind-set. Mixing business suits with cowboy boots sends the nonverbal message that you are foremost a cowboy/cowgirl, interacting and fitting in best in that region only.

The Santa Fe look also luxuriates in popularity, even outside the Southwest. It is especially big in the art world. In that element, the look can create an aura of creativity and mystique. Outside of that sphere, if this is adopted on a consistent basis, regional pigeonholing will occur, limiting other opportunities that might come to you.

Once you are placed "in a box," it takes time to get out. Think for a moment about Hawaiian shirts or Hawaiian prints. When worn on the mainland for business pursuits, they look silly and out of place. I am not opposed to expressing love and respect for any geographical region, culture, or race, with particular clothing or accessories. Just be careful of placing unnecessary, self-imposed limitations upon yourself by choosing regional or ethnic dress in your *professional* life.

With the telecommunications technology available to us now, our world is shrinking — not in mileage — but in accessibility. We are becoming a global society, as more and more companies are doing business internationally. Economic experts claim that we will see the scope of global business increase greatly over our lifetime. This makes it all the more important to have a wardrobe that will take you anywhere in the world and allow you to command respect.

Demonstrate your brilliance by building a world-class business wardrobe that includes empowering casual attire. By owning a few right pieces, you can create magic in your closet, whether you are traveling or working at home. Be sure to read Chapters 5 and 6, "Empowering Business Casual Essentials," for women and men. In each section there is a gender-specific list of those essential magic pieces that do wonders with any wardrobe. Whether you are male or female, by owning these right pieces you can dramatically increase your dress IQ.

JACKET POWER:

Jackets head the list of magical garments. Upgrading almost any outfit, a distinctive jacket promotes you as a force to be taken seriously. Quality jackets — clean, pressed, and in excellent condition — add authority and power. Ill-fitting, wrinkled, shabby jackets covered with pet hair or dandruff downgrade you as any garment in bad condition does.

Statistics show that when a man is wearing a dress shirt and tie, people assume he has a suit jacket or sport coat nearby, either in his office or car. Unfortunately, the same is not assumed about a woman who is not wearing a jacket.

A high-quality, dark-colored, well-tailored jacket is critical to a Business Casual wardrobe for both women and men. Notice the emphasis on premier quality. Meeting these criteria, a jacket is the pivotal point of your business wardrobe.

Determine your best power-neutral color before buying. Power colors are dark in tone. Black and navy are the front-runners of empowering hues and are great coordinates to mix and match with your existing pieces.

POWER-NEUTRAL COLOR CHART

Black

Navy

Dark Gray

Brown

Choose the neutral color that clicks with you. Then purchase a longer-cut, stylish jacket in this tone. No boxy, shapeless jackets are allowed because those types put you behind, not ahead, in the game of business. A perfect fit is essential. It looks comfortable, it is comfortable, and it adds a sense of style to your overall silhouette.

To gain the edge, keep a jacket available to you at all times. Wear one every day of your business schedule. Even if you take it off later, keep it handy for the unexpected. Opportunity often knocks at inopportune times. Be ready and always demonstrate casual smarts.

THE CAPSULE WARDROBE:
MAGICAL GARMENTS THAT GET YOU AHEAD

These magical pieces multiply your wardrobe dollars, simplify the act of getting dressed, and are guaranteed to command respect. This core wardrobe allows you to look entirely different even when you wear the same jacket, trousers, or skirt several times in one week. Antiquated rules thrown away, it is okay to repeat wearing certain garments. If they look extraordinary on you, this is certainly true, especially while you're in build-a-wardrobe mode.

Focus initially on one neutral color family for your basic pieces. Choose your best power neutral from the chart on page 92 and purchase a solid-colored suit that is flattering to you in this color. Also purchase one pair of shoes in that color. This plan simplifies accessories and shopping.

Each garment should be stunning, yet simple. Stick with classic designs; gimmicky fashions are too memorable for repeat wearing. This does not mean that you should buy solemn, boring, frumpy, outdated apparel. Each piece should have eye appeal and interesting lines, and be current but not faddish. Purchase the highest quality you can possibly afford. (Chapter 8 shows how to recognize quality; the price is not always a barometer.)

It is passé, actually irresponsible, to have your closets stuffed full of unnecessary clothing. The capsule wardrobe is in. Consisting of a few essential garments that work well together, the capsule wardrobe is a delight for the white-collar worker and the business traveler, or for a tight budget. In many cases, even those who have excess money to spend on clothing have adopted this minimalist approach to dressing.

THE CAPSULE WARDROBE
A capsule wardrobe that gets you ahead embodies the following criteria:

- **QUALITY GARMENTS** — Always, always, always, buy quality over quantity.

- **STYLISH, YET SIMPLE GARMENTS** — No novelty-driven pieces as part of the core. Those kinds of items are extras that can be added later. Current, classic styles preferred.

- **IMPECCABLE FIT** — Each garment in this core group must be well tailored and fit you perfectly. The correct fit is comfortable and appears comfortable on you. If you fidget, tug, or pull on a garment, it does not fit properly. See a reputable tailor or alterations person for correct fit.

- **COLOR COORDINATED IN A DARK NEUTRAL HUE** — For ultimate flexibility, this is a critical ingredient to the capsule. Brighter alternative colors can be added. For you to command respect and radiate personal power, the basic pieces must all be a neutral color.

Power Casual Capsule Wardrobe, Female:

She already owns:

- Black suit, two-piece, in fine wool, medium to lightweight; jacket is longer-cut; skirt is straight-lined and short

- Blouse, black and white zebra print, long-sleeve

FIG. 4:1 PIECES SHE ALREADY OWNS

To create several Power Casual outfits with her existing pieces (listed on page 94), she would add these items to complete this capsule:

FIG. 4:2 POWER CASUAL PIECES TO ADD TO HER CAPSULE WARDROBE

- **Slacks** — Black, in similar fabric as the suit jacket
- **Top** — Black, long-sleeve, in LYCRA, wool, silk, etc.
- **Second Jacket** — Longer cut, semifitted, in any color that looks rich with black
- **Belt** — Black leather or suede with buckle in gold or silver-tone metal
- **Earrings** — One pair; metal and black combo (metal coordinates with the belt buckle)
- **Necklace** — Metal that coordinates with belt buckle and earrings
- **Scarf** — Silk, long style (not square), any colors as long as it has some black in the design

She can then choose between these six simple, powerful, elegant, outfits:

■ **Pantsuit Effect with Jacket**

All black can look very rich layered together. The top is tucked into the slacks and topped with a belt, or it can be worn with the top out (not tucked in) and belted over the top. Accessorize with a necklace and earrings, or just earrings. You may also add a scarf with other colors, but it must have some black in it. Do not wear a necklace if you are adding a scarf; save that to create a different outfit.

FIG. 4:3 PANTSUIT EFFECT WITH JACKET

FIG. 4:4 ALL BLACK-DRESS EFFECT WITH NO JACKET

■ **All Black-Dress Effect with No Jacket***

The black top is tucked into the black skirt and topped with a belt. Accessorize with a necklace and earrings. Wear opaque stockings and low-heel shoes for a Dressy Casual look. *This works well for the svelte figure. If you carry extra weight, wear either of the two jackets for this look. The alternate-colored jacket will look more casual than the black jacket; both are casually chic.

FIG. 4:5 DRESS EFFECT WITH SECOND JACKET

■ **Dress Effect with Second Jacket**

Same basic ensemble as shown in the previous photograph, but this outfit is finished with the alternate-colored jacket.

FIG. 4:6 PANTSUIT 2

■ Pantsuit 2

This outfit consists of black trousers worn with the zebra print blouse and the black jacket. The blouse is tucked into the slacks and belted for a finished look, especially if you want to remove your jacket. Complete the ensemble with earrings. A necklace is optional, depending upon the neckline of your top.

■ Pantsuit 3 — Jumpsuit Effect*

Here we have the black top, the black trousers, and the black belt. Wear the earrings. A necklace can also be worn. To create a different outfit, wear a scarf at the neck instead of a necklace.

*This look also works best for the svelte figure.

**FIG. 4:7 PANTSUIT 3 –
JUMPSUIT EFFECT**

**FIG. 4:8 PANTSUIT 4 – JUMPSUIT
EFFECT W/ALTERNATE JACKET**

■ Pantsuit 4 — Jumpsuit with the Alternate-Colored Jacket

This look is the same as Pantsuit 3 with the addition of the second jacket. The outfit may be changed further by adding a necklace or a scarf.

Six outfits from so few basic pieces? Yes, and there are other possible combinations. **The outfits shown in Figures 4:9, 4:10, and 4:11 are additional variations from this same capsule.**

And you can change these same outfits even more by adding different shoes, belt, and scarf. How about the basic black outfit (Figure 4:7 on page 97) worn with brown crocodile shoes and belt, and finished with a scarf that has brown and black colors in it? Simple accessories can make the same coordinates look like new outfits.

FIG. 4:9 CAPSULE VARIATION W/JACKET AND PRINT BLOUSE

FIG. 4:10 CAPSULE VARIATION W/SHORT SKIRT AND PRINT BLOUSE

You can also add other casual separates to create even more outfits with the core capsule. Remember, the core capsule consists of the black suit, black-and-white zebra-print blouse, black pants, black top, and red jacket. The separate items shown to the left all work with the core capsule garments to create innumerable outfits. Three outfit variations created from these additional pieces and the core capsule garments are shown in Figures 4:13, 4:14, and 4:15.

FIG. 4:11 CAPSULE VARIATION W/BLACK PANTS AND PRINT BLOUSE

FIG. 4:12 CASUAL PIECES TO SUPPORT HER CAPSULE WARDROBE

FIG. 4:13 CAPSULE VARIATION ADDING COLOR TO BLACK

FIG. 4:15 CAPSULE VARIATION W/GRAY TURTLENECK

Wearing any of these combinations, you are world-class chic *wherever* you may be going, especially if you have purchased high-quality fabrics. When your budget allows, enlarge this capsule wardobe by adding another suit, such as the brown suit in Figure 4:16. A suit in any color family that coordinates with your existing black or navy pieces — as long as the color looks good on *you* — is an excellent choice.

FIG. 4:14 CAPSULE VARIATION W/CASUAL SEPARATES

A capsule wardrobe plan can be built around any color combination. Start with your best power-neutral color for your basic garments, then add other hues that are complementary to your natural coloring and that coordinate well with your best neutral. This plan ensures that you are assembling a capsule wardrobe that works hard for you professionally and socially.

FIG. 4:16   BROWN SUIT

FIG. 4:17 BLACK PINSTRIPE
PANTSUIT

These examples are of pantsuits in black and gray that a capsule could be built around; all are excellent choices for the take-me-seriously millennium woman.

FIG. 4:18 GRAY PANTSUIT

FIG. 4:19 OUTFIT ABOVE,
WITHOUT JACKET

FIG. 4:20 PIECES HE ALREADY OWNS

Power Casual, Capsule Wardrobe, Male:

He already owns:

- Suit, navy, three-button in fine tropical wool, trousers are pleated and cuffed
- Collared knit shirt
- Black shoes, dressy slip-on style, all-leather, hard-sole

To create several Power Casual outfits with existing pieces, he would add these items:

- **Sport Coat** — Brown, navy, and olive multi-colored jacket. You could choose any sport coat that has navy as the dominant background
- **Alternate Trousers** — These taupe-toned dress trousers are fabricated in fine wool, and they are pleated and cuffed. The color must work with the sport coat and with the navy suit jacket. Choose a neutral color accordingly (charcoal, dark taupe, dark gray, olive, etc.).
- **Shirt** — Red point collar that coordinates with navy and with the colors of the sport jacket and alternate trousers. The shirt you choose

FIG. 4:21 POWER CASUAL PIECES HE WOULD ADD

may have a subtle pattern in a tone-on-tone manner or a coordinate color. Any high-quality shirt that does not require a tie.

- **Belt** — All-leather, black, metal-tipped end (silver tip, not too heavy).

He can then choose between these simple, yet powerful outfits:

- Navy (solid-colored) suit with gray knit shirt
Tipped black belt
Black slip-on shoes with patterned socks

FIG. 4:22 NAVY SUIT W/
GRAY KNIT SHIRT

- Navy suit with red sport shirt and no tie
Tipped black belt
Black slip-on shoes worn with coordinated patterned socks

FIG. 4:23 NAVY SUIT W/RED SHIRT
AND NO TIE

- Multicolored (navy, brown, and olive) sport jacket
  Red point-collar shirt
  Taupe suit trousers
  Tipped black belt
  Black slip-on shoes

FIG. 4:24 MULTICOLORED
SPORT JACKET W/RED SHIRT

FIG. 4:25 MULTICOLORED
SPORT JACKET W/GRAY KNIT

- Multicolored sport jacket
Taupe trousers
Knit shirt (gray)
(Same black belt and black shoes)

FIG. 4:26 NAVY SUIT JACKET W/RED SHIRT

■ Navy suit jacket
Taupe trousers
Red point-collar shirt
Tipped black belt
Black slip-on shoes

■ Gray knit shirt w/taupe trousers — navy suit jacket or no jacket optional
(Same black belt and black shoes)

FIG. 4:27 GRAY KNIT W/TAUPE TROUSERS

FIG. 4:28 RED POINT-COLLAR W/TAUPE TROUSERS

■ Red point-collar shirt with taupe trousers — no jacket or either jacket optional
Tipped belt (very important when not wearing a jacket)
Coordinated patterned socks and dressy slip-on shoes

Seven outfits from these few pieces? Yes — and even more when you consider the range of shirts you probably already have hanging in the closet. If you are on a shoestring budget, you can simply add a second pair of trousers that works with your solid suit coat, for several changes of outfits. You can add the sport jacket later — or if you need your money to go toward a second suit, then consider a microcheck in a blue/black or olive/navy combination. All these pieces can be used separately with the solid suit pieces to create many great-looking casual outfits.

You can also pair your navy suit jacket with jeans for a dressed-down, yet smart look. The key here is for the jeans to be clean and pressed, and to be worn with the hard-sole leather shoes to be truly casually smart.

If you are blessed with abundant finances, create two or three capsule wardrobes in different color families. Adding variety and flexibility, this multiple approach gives you all the advantages of easy dressing and traveling.

FIG. 4:29 GRAY SUIT
W/BLACK SHIRT

FIG. 4:30 GRAY TROUSERS
W/BLACK JACKET

A potent capsule is shown here: a black four-button suit mixed with various pieces, such as gray trousers, a blue shirt, and a gray shirt. These combinations command respect and they send a strong message. All of these outfits proclaim success and they say, *"I'm a serious player in the game of business."*

FIG. 4:31 GRAY TROUSERS
W/BLUE SHIRT

CLOSET SAVVY: THE WORK STATION THAT PRODUCES RESULTS FOR YOU

Another aspect of a high image IQ is closet smarts. Closet arrangement can save you valuable time or waste it unnecessarily. Dressing down highlights the problem of using separates. You can be all over the closet trying to find this or that garment for a casual outfit. Poor arrangement of clothing leads to another efficiency pitfall: failure to maximize the use of all wearable garments. Most people do not utilize the garments they already own to their fullest capacity, so they don't get their money's worth from clothing they've already purchased.

In my consulting business, I have done hundreds (probably thousands) of wardrobes, and I have found an amusing common phenomenon. Unless they are wearing a suit, most people stand at their closet door expecting a great outfit to magically jump out at them. When it doesn't, they choose the same old coordinates or an unflattering outfit, out of frustration. My clients are amazed at how many great-looking outfits I can create from their existing pieces. They simply have not noticed them, due to their closet disorder.

A jumbled closet makes for jumbled-looking ensembles. Jumbled closets lead to bumbled efforts to put separates together easily.

Restructuring Your Closet

Step 1. Remove all clothing you have not worn in one year.

If you really want to get organized, make that six months. Donate them to your favorite charity or take them to a resale shop. This is a very important step; it can change your life. All these useless garments take up space in your mind. Get them out of your closet (you're not wearing them anyway).

If you feel sentimental about some of these items that you know you will never wear again, create a special Sentimental Section. Hang them in the back of the closet, away from your daily wear. Do not keep more than three to four items here. If your closet is tiny, limit it to two items.

Novelty pieces can go into a Costume Area. You have a problem if your Special Sections occupy more room in your closet than your professional or daily garments do. If that is the case, consider going into the costume rental business. Otherwise, get real and pare it down.

Step 2. Discard all tired, outdated items, even if you are wearing them right now.

Tired clothes make you look wrung-out and lifeless. If you are hanging on to things that are outdated just because you loved them way back when, McSly has reared its ugly head.

People often keep items from college or some other positive phase in their lives. Beware! Such attachment keeps you stuck in the past. You are not living in the present, allowing your current life to be all it can be. As your closet is, so is your mind — and then, so is your life!

Step 3. Get rid of all items that you know look disastrous on you.
Don't listen to McSly's chatter. Take three deep breaths and DO IT!

Step 4. Divide your closet into two sections — one section for spring/summer and another for fall/winter. Depending on where you live, you may have many items that can be worn year-round or that are transitional pieces. Just keep those available in your working closet and move the off-season definites.

If it is possible to keep your off-season garments in a separate closet or area away from your daily closet, all the better. But I realize this is not always possible.

Workstation Closet Arrangement: (Women)
■ **Hang all the jackets together.**
This includes separating suit jackets from their skirts. You may be amazed what other items those suit jackets can be worn with to create exciting new outfits, especially Business Casual outfits.
■ **Hang all the skirts together.**
Sort them by lengths, hanging all the short ones together and then the longer ones consecutively.
■ **Hang all the pants together.**
Yes, even those that came with a jacket or specific outfit. Separate the dressier pants from corduroys or more casual fabrics.
■ **Hang all the tops and blouses together.**
Separate them according to sleeveless, short sleeve, and long sleeve. Then arrange them according to fabrics, within the sleeve length sections — silks, cottons, LYCRA, etc.
■ **Hang all the vests or novelty items together.**
■ **Hang all the jeans together, the shorts together, etc.**
■ **Keep all the sweaters together.**
Most sweaters are best kept folded, but keep them together. Hang those that can be hung without damaging them.

Now go back through each section and arrange the items according to color family. Follow the same plan for your playwear. All T-shirts should be hung together, for instance. Yes, *hanging*, if at all possible, to reduce wrinkling.

Now it is easy to create new outfits by taking a jacket sleeve and running it across your other sections. Start with any piece — a blouse, a skirt, pants — and pull it across the other garments to find coordinates. Check for fabric mixes, color blending, and coordination to see what might work together with another item. Try the pieces on, then view carefully (in good lighting) to determine whether or not the ensemble is truly a great outfit on *you*.

Workstation Closet Arrangement: (Men)
■ **Hang all the suits together.**
Examine each suit to determine if the jacket can legitimately double as a sport coat. If so, hang those types together with the matching pants, just behind the coat in the Suit Section. You'll find more information on which jackets can double as sport coats in Chapter 6. Most solids can, also microchecks, etc. Pinstripes cannot; they are strictly suits.
■ **Hang all the dress shirts together.**
Separate the shirts into color families (all whites, blues, etc.). Within each color family, separate the French cuffs from the button cuffs, and separate varying collars such as banded, tabs, button-downs, etc.
■ **Hang all the sport shirts together.**
Again, sort out the color families, then sort them by collars, etc.
■ **Hang all the knit shirts together.**
Use the same procedure as for the other shirts .
■ **Hang all the dress trousers together (not the suit pants).**
■ **Hang all the sporty trousers together.**
This section includes all khakis, all cotton pants, elastic-waist pants, drawstring waist pants, cargo-style pants, and corduroy pants, etc.
■ **Hang all the jeans together.**
■ **Hang all the vests together.**
■ **Keep all the sweaters together.**
These are usually best folded, but keep them all together.
■ **Hang all the T-shirts together.**
T-shirts will be less wrinkled if they are hanging, instead of folded. If you have the space, hang them, at least your favorites.
■ **Shorts should be hung together as well.**

If you take a jacket sleeve or shirt sleeve or trouser leg and pull it across the other sections, you can instantly see what would potentially produce a harmonious outfit. Check for fabric mixes, color blending, or coordination to see what might work together with another item. Try the pieces on, then view yourself carefully (in good lighting) to decide if the ensemble is a great outfit on *you*.

This system works if you work it. Some of you are screaming, *"Well, this is great for one afternoon, but it won't stay that way!"* Bingo! You will have to retrain yourself to hang items back in their category when you are doing the laundry or bringing home dry cleaning. It requires discipline, but it is really no different from unloading the dishwasher and putting every item in its proper place in your cabinets. The rewards of maximizing the wearing potential of your clothing and saving valuable time when getting dressed are worth the effort it takes to keep things sorted. (McSly will try to convince you otherwise.) Be wary of his whisper about how much trouble it is. If disorder takes over, don't give up — take a few minutes when you can to sort things out. Your closet will quickly return to order if you were thorough in doing the initial organization.

To muliply their wardrobe dollars, many of my clients have found it beneficial to keep a picture file of certain outfits. Either lay the coordinates on the floor, including best accessory choices, or literally put them on for the photo. Whichever way you choose, file the photos in a recipe-type box or folder, according to the outfit category. While this is initially time consuming, it saves a lot of time in your day-to-day life when you are deciding what to wear. If you have a hyperactive personal saboteur living in your closet, this is an excellent taming strategy.

Another premier arena for the damaging deeds of your McSly is the care you give your clothes. The "Health Care" of your clothing is critical in getting the most value for your money and in looking sharp. Most people are in a toxic fog about how to handle and care for their clothing, and how to foster good apparel health. Crisp, fresh clothing exudes professionalism and personal power. Worn, tired, ill-kept garments sabotage you by making *you* appear ill or exhausted.

Unsung heroes, dress-down garments are the neglected children in most closets. Most people give little care to their casual wear.

Tips to Lengthen the Life Span of Your Wardrobe Dollars:

■ Your clothes need room to breathe. Overcrowding your closet means premature death for your clothes. Leave a space between each garment. *All* fabrics need to air out. This also cuts down on wrinkles and cleaning bills. You can suffocate your clothes if you indefinitely leave them in plastic bags — especially dry-cleaner bags. The warmer and more humid the climate in your closet, the more severe the damage can be.

■ Too much dry cleaning or laundering is the biggest clothing killer. Dry-cleaning fluids, detergents, and hot irons destroy the fibers, and over time they can tire out the heart of your precious pieces. **This is not a license to wear soiled garments!** If a garment is not soiled and has no odor, often just a good airing, *proper* pressing, or lint removal makes the garment fresh and young again.

■ Cedar (bags, bars, liners, or closets) is the healthiest choice to safely store out-of-season apparel. Avoid the use of mothballs. Many people are severely allergic to the formaldehyde that saturates mothballs. Who knows, the clothes may be, also! And the smell is suspiciously similar to embalming fluid.

■ Affection and TLC are primary needs for clothing, too. Your clothes have pride. When you first undress, your clothing retains a slight moisture and heat from being *so-o-o* intimate with *your* body. Throwing your clothes on the floor or in a pile gives the garment no chance for dignity. Have mercy, please!

Giving you energy and confidence, the right clothing is like a great friend. As a valuable tool and significant support system, the right garments can lift you up to attain greater levels of success. Beware of any saboteur activity in your daily habits of handling and caring for your clothing — dress-down and dress-up garments alike. Maintain them as you would a precious friendship or a prime investment of costly real estate.

"The battle
for women's rights
has been
largely won."

— Margaret Thatcher

Empowering
Business Casual Essentials
for Women

Approaching the millennium, it is an exciting time to be alive and to be a woman on Planet Earth. As women, we now have opportunities to excel in being and doing more than ever in history.

Even though it is common worldwide for women to hold positions of power in politics and in business, the corporate glass ceiling remains intact for many businesswomen. Gender inequality remains a problem even though a woman may possess the same or greater expertise, and may work just as many hours as her male cohorts. Many professional women still have to swim upstream in shark-infested waters regarding their salaries and benefits.

Fortunately, we live in a time when even the Berlin Wall can come down. I challenge the men and women of this age to do their part to make the ceiling obsolete. This chapter is dedicated to bringing down the glass ceiling, once and for all.

For this to occur, women cannot afford to be indifferent about their professional image. Nor can they indulge in sloppiness, extremely casual clothing, or poor grooming. Even when it is Dress-Way-Down Day, a woman can wear no attire more relaxed than that in the *Smart Casual* category. *Business Casual, Dressy Casual,* and *Smart Casual* are the only dress-down images that have any glass-shattering capabilities. Most cultures remain basically patriarchal with the male reigning as the dominant workforce icon. Thatcher said the battle was *largely* won, not completely won.

Wearing *excessively* casual attire in the workplace quickly disempowers women. Women are far more easily stripped of personal power by inappropriate apparel and grooming than men are. In our society, men's clothing has been imbued with power and authority ("*Who wears the **pants** in the family?*").

Suffused with simpler, naturally tailored lines, men's traditional business attire has been the model for power and authority for centuries. Does this mean that women have to look like men and wear masculine clothing to succeed in business? NO! (I am adamant about this.) Nevertheless, some principles of traditional male business attire can be applied to create a stylish "Dressed Down/Up Success Formula" for women in business. Andre Maurois said, *"Business is a combination between war and sport."* Whether we are fighting wars or playing sports, we need the right strategies and the appropriate gear. The same is true in business.

Competitive negotiations are common to most business dealings. This remains true even if you shun the win/lose attitudes of war and sports. A win/win attitude toward business does not mean that you cast aside your professionalism. While our free enterprise system continues, competitive products and services will exist. To survive and to succeed or get ahead, you need a jump start that sets you apart from mediocrity.

Just as packaging of a product often determines its marketability and success, your image serves as your packaging in the marketplace. Smart professional attire imprints your demeanor and overall visual image with power and confidence, giving you a competitive edge. This is particularly important when you are dressed down. Business Casual attire draws significantly from the traditional professional dress paradigm. When one strays from this model with too relaxed apparel, demise enters like a malignant tumor silently growing in your psyche and career. Remember in the definition of Business Casual, personal power and professionalism are never sacrificed.

PRINCIPLE I. VERTICAL DRESSING = A POWERFUL, PROFESSIONAL SILHOUETTE

> *"Nature says to a woman: Be beautiful if you can, wise if you want to, but be respected, that is essential."* — Beaumarchais

In mythology and psychology, vertical lines (as in phallic symbols) are associated with power. Whether it is despised or loved, abused or used appropriately, power commands respect. Power can destroy just as surely as torrential rains. Power can do good just as surely as timely, gentle rain produces growth. Remember, power is simply the "ability to do."

In many of the Eastern religions and cultures, warrior-like masculine energy (whether in a male or female body) is referred to as "Yang," often depicted as a vertical line. By design, not accidentally, men's conventional business wear has utilized vertical lines to purposefully add a sense of power. Whether male or female, real or illusionary vertical lines in clothing make a person appear taller and slimmer. This result is far more desirable than appearing shorter and wider, which occurs when the horizontal perspective is accented.

A strong vertical effect visually increases your personal power. Men's traditional business styles have capitalized on the vertical-dressing principle and embodied empowerment with garments such as:

- Ties (the most famous vertical in men's wear)
- Suits (long jackets with full-length trousers)
- Pinstripes and chalk striping in suit fabrics
- Braces (suspenders)
- Long sleeves in jackets and shirts.

These vertical visual designs enhance the wearer's personal power by making one appear taller, slimmer, and more authoritative. How does this translate for women's clothing? Can a woman use the same principle and remain true to her inherent feminine image and power? Yes, she can, and she can do so without wearing masculine suits and ties.

Womanized Verticals — Business Casual Pointers

Straight skirts — long or short. Slim-lined long skirts are an instant vertical. When you are wearing short skirts, coordinate your stocking and shoe color to match or blend or to be one shade darker than your hem length to create a strong vertical. Straight-lined does not mean too tight.

Wear black, brown, nude, or navy hose when coordinating your hosiery to a shorter hem length. On the whole, colored hose such as green, purple, red, etc. are unacceptable for the workplace, when they are paired with a short skirt. Conversely, dark-green hose worn with a long green skirt or pants and dark-green shoes look fabulous and are professionally chic.

FIG. 5:2 *black short, straight skirt w/black hose and black shoes*

FIG. 5:3 *double-breasted jacket that tapers slightly at the waist*

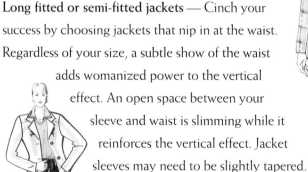

Long fitted or semi-fitted jackets — Cinch your success by choosing jackets that nip in at the waist. Regardless of your size, a subtle show of the waist adds womanized power to the vertical effect. An open space between your sleeve and waist is slimming while it reinforces the vertical effect. Jacket sleeves may need to be slightly tapered.

FIG. 5:4 *long, fitted jacket worn buttoned and worn open*

Avoid boxy, shapeless jackets because they widen you, creating a horizontal line in your mid-torso area.

FIG. 5:5 *boxy jacket*

JACKET ALTERATION DO'S:

1. Nip in the waist at side seams

2. Taper sleeves to create space between arms and waist

Short jackets — Adding an air of power to your physical silhouette, jackets are always an excellent choice with a Business Casual outfit. We've already applauded the slimming, vertical aspects of long semi-fitted jackets. Short jackets also score in the vertical game when they are paired with long skirts or pants. Their vertical effect is most potent when in the same color family as the skirt or pants.

When you are wearing a short jacket in a contrasting, complementary color, keep the additional outfit pieces in identical color tones (relative to each other) to ensure a slimming, empowering vertical result. Note the details in the short jacket illustrations that typify this point.

FIG. 5:6 *short jacket worn with pants in the same color family and short jacket in green worn with a long black skirt and black top*

FIG. 5:7 *classic trousers with cuffs and without cuffs*

FIG. 5:8 *slim-leg trousers and wide-leg pants*

Trousers and Slim-Leg Pants

Pants naturally create a bold vertical. In most companies, pants are acceptable as Business Casual attire for women. Actually, all pants — even the nicest daytime pantsuits — fall into the casual category for women in the workplace. Avoid any form of bell-bottom pants when you are heading for the office, even on a weekend. Extremely wide-leg pants should also be avoided for business unless they are paired with a long jacket or a long tunic top.

Rule of thumb for pant length: The wider the leg, the longer the pant must be to be slenderizing. The tapered slim-leg pants can be worn slightly shorter. For instance, the cigarette-leg pants should hit just below the ankle bone.

FIG. 5:9 *cigarette pants, very tapered*

PANT(ING) NO-NO'S FOR WOMEN WHO MEAN BUSINESS:

- No capri pants — they communicate leisure time.
- No pants that are too tight, regardless of style.
- No panty lines or body-suit lines should show.
- No stirrup pants with the stirrup showing. That look is passé.
- No pants that are too short. If it hits on your calf, it is not appropriate for business.

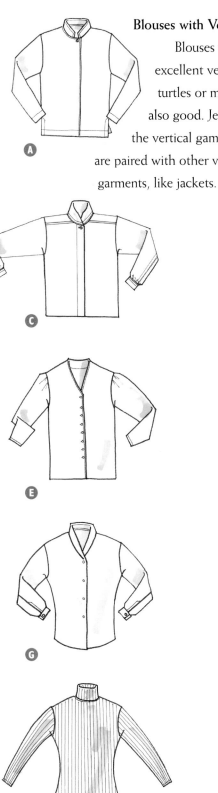

Blouses with Vertical Appeal

Blouses with pointed collars create an excellent vertical visual. Turtlenecks, mock turtles or mandarin collars, and V-necks are also good. Jewel necklines can play the vertical game when they are paired with other vertical garments, like jackets.

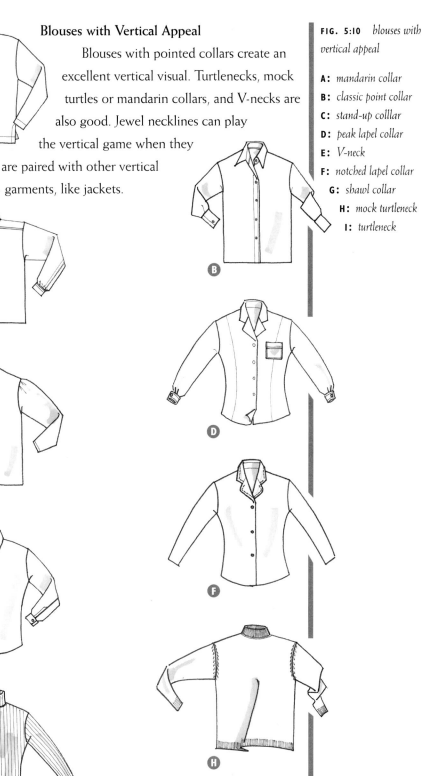

FIG. 5:10 *blouses with vertical appeal*

A: *mandarin collar*
B: *classic point collar*
C: *stand-up colllar*
D: *peak lapel collar*
E: *V-neck*
F: *notched lapel collar*
G: *shawl collar*
H: *mock turtleneck*
I: *turtleneck*

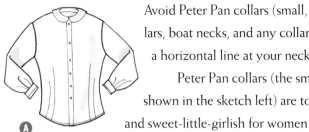

Avoid Peter Pan collars (small, rounded), square collars, boat necks, and any collar or neckline that creates a horizontal line at your neck or shoulders.

Peter Pan collars (the small rounded collar shown in the sketch left) are too wimpy and sweet-little-girlish for women who are serious about business. Square collars look too nautical, sending a sailor-girl communication. Both collars are fine on young girls, but are certainly not the preferred statement for a professional woman.

The boat neck is a great neckline for the narrow-shouldered woman in her recreation time, but not for business. This style creates a strong horizontal line at the shoulder, which defeats the vertical effect, and it will make you look shorter.

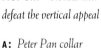

FIG. 5:11 *blouses that defeat the vertical appeal*

A: *Peter Pan collar*
B: *square collar*
C: *boat neck collar*

Shoulder pads — are necessary to add power to a woman's physique, but not Shoulder Pads on Steroids! Avoid the huge extended pads of the '80s. The newer, smaller pads strengthen the shoulders in a believable style. They also balance your hipline and lengthen your torso, making your figure look more proportional.

Long scarves — Be careful about overdoing scarves, but oblong scarves are an excellent way to add a vertical touch of pattern or color. Avoid square scarves; they can be frumpy.

FIG. 5:12 *empowering oblong scarf*

Long sleeves — ALWAYS, even if you roll them up or push them up to a shorter length.

FIG. 5:13 *two vertical-effect sleeve lengths: long sleeves and long sleeves pushed up*

FIG. 5:14 *short sleeves add a horizontal line — destroys vertical effect*

FIG. 5:15 MID-HEEL PUMP

Heels — Mid-heel pumps add height, increasing your vertical appearance. Don't go to extremes with this and wear spike or stiletto heels in the workplace. You will not be taken seriously as a businesswoman (unless you aspire to be CEO of a bordello).

Monochromatic dressing — Identical color or shades of the same hue. Wear the darker tones on the bottom with lighter tones higher, around the face. This makes you look taller, slimmer, and coordinated. When the fabrics ooze with high quality and rich color tones, a well-accessorized, monochromatic ensemble conveys success — money in the bank in present time.

shades of olive business casual ensemble

Paradoxically, some obvious verticals that are common to women's wear do not serve you well in business pursuits. These glamorous verticals disempower you and your goals in the workplace:

■ **Long, dangle earrings** — Save these to enjoy for evenings or time off.
■ **Long, long hair** (Mega-inches beyond shoulder length) — This does not mean that a woman cannot have long hair. If so, she must pull it back, put it up, or cut it to shoulder length, or a few inches below the shoulders for a professional look.

PRINCIPLE II. SUBTLE USE OF COLOR = POWERFUL, PROFESSIONAL, CHIC IMAGE

"Good taste is the feminine of genius." – Edward Fitzgerald

The classic model of professional dress does not embrace vast amounts of color. Color is not absent; it is just carefully utilized. Women can enjoy wearing brightly colored suits, such as royal blue, purple, green, and red, and still be crisply professional. The trick is not to overdo color at one time. For instance, when you are wearing a royal blue suit, accessorize with black to enhance the suit's power. Forgo the matching royal blue shoes for business.

Those brightly colored jackets make wonderful Business Casual outfits when paired with coordinated neutrals as a backdrop. Keep in mind that dark neutrals and solid-colored, dark tones of bright hues are the strongest "power" colors for Business Casual attire.

Business Casual Chic Color Guide for Women

Beyond a single hue, **two-color outfits** work best for a professional casual look for women. Introduce a third color or more by use of a scarf or pin. The exception here would be a multicolored blouse, and then you want the main background color to obviously coordinate with your other pieces.

FIG. 5:17 *two-color outfit*

In the first drawing, her knit skirt and knit top are black. To look taller and create a stronger vertical, she chose black pumps and sheer black hose. For a dynamic addition of color to the solid-black backdrop, she added a red jacket. Notice that the jacket is the longer cut, which strengthens the vertical effect and is slimming.

FIG. 5:18 *basic two-color outfit with subtle addition of a third color*

In the second example, she kept her basic pieces the same. To create a different outfit, she wore the same red jacket buttoned and subtly introduced a third color (purple) with the red-black-purple scarf.

FIG. 5:19 *three-color outfit*

In the following drawing, she has worn the same black skirt and red jacket. This time she has worn a white sheared, V-neck blouse under the jacket. A white blouse is classic. You can wear it with almost any ensemble of businesslike separates and have an empowered classic look.

A two-color style creates such an empowering silhouette that it merits another look. Examine the nuances of these two-color outfits:

Taupe-colored silk pants worn with a matching silk T-shirt, topped with a short, black wool-crepe jacket show another example of a dynamite two-colored Business Casual outfit. Pants and top are accented with a thin taupe leather belt with a pewter buckle. A short necklace in silver with an inset onyx stone and silver-and-black earrings unite this ensemble. Pewter-toned metallic shoes worn with light taupe hose complete and add snap to this outfit.

In the second example, the same basic taupe garments — pants and silk T-top — are worn with a longer-cut royal blue jacket. The belt is dark taupe leather with a brushed gold buckle. The brushed gold earrings complement the belt buckle, as well as the buttons on the jacket. A short scarf (in blue, gold, and taupe) tied at the neck unites this ensemble. Dark taupe pumps worn with skin-toned hose complete this two-color outfit.

Three-color outfits can be professional, if they are carefully put together.

This ensemble combines several colors, but it is still rich and sophisticated. The solid-black pants are the base for her paisley blouse. The touches of black in the blouse give credibility to the black pants. The green jacket picks up the background color of the multicolored blouse. Her shoes and hose are in the same tone as her pants. This adds to her rich, pulled-together look. She reeks with casual chic!

Harmonize shoes and hose with each outfit. Be meticulous about this.

- **Shoes should be as dark or darker than the color of your hem length** to increase the vertical effect. (It's the most slimming also.) *Never wear light hose and dark shoes with a dark dress or skirt. This little-girlish look communicates that you have the mindset of a 10-year-old.*

- **Black shoes and black hose can be worn with navy,** especially midnight or dark navy. Navy tones are difficult to match in leather and suede. Dark navy clothing looks better with black shoes than with medium-to-light navy or royal navy shoes.

- **Avoid all brightly colored hosiery for the workplace.** For example: A red suit is best worn with a smoky gray, taupe, sheer black, or flesh-toned hose with black, dark gray, brown, or daytime metallic shoes (never red hose and red shoes. Look to the buttons on the jacket for hints on best accessory colors.

- **Daytime metallic shoes are great neutrals** to wear with bright colors, white, and beige. (Not evening-shiny metallic.) Avoid white shoes in the workplace, even if you are wearing white clothing.

Monochromatic dressing — Separate garments in the same color or varying shades of the same hue can create dynamic casual outfits. This style of dressing also rates as a distinct "vertical." Generally, this type of outfit makes you appear pulled together. Unless the fabrics are cheap, this subtle look exudes richness. Remember, when you dress as if you have already achieved some level of success, more success is attracted to you!

FIG. 5:23 *power casual monochromatic outfit*

Accessories used to complete this outfit:
- Belt – wine-colored suede with matte silver buckle
- Earrings – antique silver with old coin inset
- Bracelet – wrist cuff in matte silver
- Necklace – long matte silver rope chain, worn doubled
- Shoes – suede boots, mid-calf in burgundy tones
- Hosiery – textured burgundy opaque or plain sheer stockings

All of her garments are variations of the same hue: a cabernet wine color. The overall effect is smashing. Furthermore, she is extremely comfortable in the long, knit wrap skirt and knit turtleneck. Note that the skirt is a darker hue than the top, which helps to elongate her and bring focus to her face. The jacket adds power and enhances the pulled-together look by picking up both color tones — the darker jacket body and the lighter-toned velvet lapels and cuffs. Her casual boots add flair as do the antique silver jewelry pieces that coordinate with the buttons on her jacket. She exudes casual power!

Let's examine further the components of monochromatic styling and take an in-depth look at the outfit previously shown in the "Vertical Section."

Note the differing fabrics and textures used to create this rich and powerful olive outfit. Each item is an outstanding garment on its own, and they create an interesting, empowering look when coordinated together.

Accessories used to complete this outfit:
- Belt – olive-green suede with burnished gold buckle
- Earrings – burnished gold
- Bracelet – burnished gold
- Shoes – dark olive suede pumps
- Hosiery – patterned olive knee-highs or panty hose

FIG. 5:24 *power casual monochromatic outfit*

Olive green wool trousers worn with a lighter-toned olive silk blouse and topped with a textured olive cardigan-style jacket make for a beautiful outfit. Her jewelry complements the burnished gold on her belt buckle. She is exceptionally well put together. She has flair and style, and she absolutely exudes casual power. Dark olive suede boots and patterned olive-on-olive hosiery (the pattern shows only at the foot/ankle area) add richness and high-class polish to complete this wow outfit.

She could opt for olive suede boots or bronze metallic shoes, as well as black or dark brown. If wearing black, brown, or bronze shoes, choose a hose color in tone with the shoe, forgoing a pattern.

Wearing either of these empowering monochromatic outfits, she can easily go from the casual workplace to the airport where a client will be meeting her for an informal meeting before boarding the plane. Then she can go on to her destination in comfort, arriving at the hotel looking fabulous, ready to join an associate for a quick drink and a next-day-agenda meeting.

While we are exploring the magic of monochromatic dressing, let's take a look at another outfit, which is made up of more casual separates than the first two ensembles.

This gray outfit is more informal — more relaxed, more dressed down — than the olive or wine-colored outfits. It typifies Rule #1 of monochromatic dressing: Always wear the darker shades on the bottom and use the lighter tones around the face to appear slimmer and taller.

She has chosen dark gray, slim-leg jean pants and a lighter gray sweater set. Even her blouse is a pale gray, which helps to define her face. Her belt buckle is a matte silver and her soft-soled loafers sport a matte silver bar across the top. It does not show in this drawing, but she is wearing tiny silver earrings as well. She finished off her gray ensemble with gray ribbed hosiery socks. She is casually smart, and she is ready for the dressed-down workplace. This outfit typifies a Smart Casual outfit that is appropriate for a young graphic designer on casual day. People working in creative industries can dress in a more relaxed manner.

FIG. 5:25 *monochromatic all gray ensemble*

Misuse of Color

Example: Yellow blouse paired with a royal blue skirt, topped with a bright, lime green/orange/yellow/light-blue print jacket. The jacket pushes the limits of workplace attire anyway, but the *big* mistake is the yellow blouse and the royal blue skirt worn with it. In this outfit, "you" cannot be seen easily. People see a barrage of color before they see you, if they see *you* at all.

When you wear a bright jacket, wear solid-colored coordinated pieces underneath to add professionalism. For example, if she had worn a solid navy blouse and navy skirt or pants with this jacket, she might have looked quite dynamic — as shown in the How-to-Correct illustration. In this example, solid navy pieces create a subtle vertical backdrop for the bright jacket. Pants would lengthen the backdrop even more than the skirt, strengthening the vertical lines of the outfit. Reducing the jarring effect of the neon mix of colors in the jacket, the solid-colored backdrop makes the overall look more acceptable for the workplace.

Additional color hazards: Avoid color-block everything! Jackets, skirts, pants, and handbags. You know the ones, red on one quarter, orange on another, then green opposite the red, and a square of blue adjacent to the orange, etc. These items simply do not make a professional statement.

Redheads tend to wear a lot of color at once. They, more than any other hair color, can get away with it in a professional setting. Often, it actually suits them.

In this multicolored outfit, she looks fun and approachable. She is still professional. She is not clownish. The white top is what makes this outfit work for business pursuits. If she had picked up another hue from the skirt for the blouse color — or even used the pink — it would have been *to-o-o* much color for the workplace.

Even for you redheads, simplicity in the use of color will always look more professional. Just as you would decorate your office to have an aura of professionalism, so it goes when you bedeck yourself for the workplace.

FIG. 5:26 *misuse of color example*

FIG. 5:27 *"how-to-correct" example*

FIG. 5:28 *multicolored outfit*

Principle III. Important-Looking, Simple Jewelry = A Powerful, Professional Demeanor

"You cannot fly like an eagle with the wings of a wren."
– William Henry Hudson

An empowered, casual silhouette demands important-looking accessories. Keep them simple, yet rich. Your jewelry should make a significant statement, making you appear intriguing and successful. This tenet is even more important when you dress down. The following guidelines have supported many businesswomen in achieving greater heights. Clasp on enhanced demeanor and greater success with these pointers.

Business Casual Jewelry Checklist for Women

Metal watch — Yes, it can be in a feminine style, but it should be silver or gold, or a combination. Metal communicates a strength that leather bands just can't muster. When dressing down, do not change from your metal watch to a leather or cloth band. Remember, this is the time to "power up" in subtle ways while you power down with your clothing.

Buy the best, most expensive watch you can possibly purchase; go for the real thing, i.e., sterling silver, platinum, 14K gold. Choose the metal tone that you most prefer in earrings and additional jewelry items. It is not mandatory to wear a watch, but if you do, it must at least *look* expensive.

FIG. 5:29 A SAMPLING OF EMPOWERING EARRINGS

FIG. 5:30 MORE EMPOWERING EARRINGS

Expensive-looking earrings — Always a must to pierce the payoff. Dressed down or up, a woman needs earrings for a completed, polished image. Earrings should accent or coordinate well with your outfit — adding a touch of power and importance to your face. Choose earrings that make an impressive statement and are flattering to your face shape. More earring styles are shown in the other jewelry photos.

Face-Shape Signposts for Selecting Empowering Earrings

- **Round and Heart-Shaped (Inverted Triangle) Faces:**

  Choose: Elongated rectangles, ovals, squares, or triangles

  Avoid: Round earrings with a circular stone or a middle that extends beyond the bezel. Also, traditional triangles that have the widest part at the bottom of the earring.

- **Square and Pear-Shaped Faces:**

  Choose: Flat round, elongated rectangle, oval, or triangular shapes.

  Avoid: Square or triangular shapes, and bulbous round shapes that extend the jawline.

- **Diamond-Shaped Faces:**

  Choose: Round, square, oval, or traditional triangular earrings.

  Avoid: Elongated rectangles, inverted triangles, and any earring with a pointy tip.

- **Oblong-Shaped (Rectangular) Faces:**

  Choose: Round, oval, or triangular shapes. Small, *short* dangles that have slight movement work well for you.

  Avoid: Elongated rectangles and inverted triangles.

- **Oval Faces:**

  Ovals can wear any shape earring successfully. Your most flattering earring depends on the size of your general features (nose, eyes, etc.), particularly your neck length and width.

- **Additional Tips:**

  – Long faces and receding chins need earrings that round out at the bottom — a wide circular shape at the bottom works well. Avoid long earrings and those that have pointy tips.

  – Faces with prominent lower cheeks or heavy jowls need earrings that are pointy at the tips — not round on the bottom, unless the earring is a long, narrow dangle that creates an obvious vertical.

  – Square jawlines should avoid earrings that extend the jawline either by width or length, such as elongated rectangles and bulging round shapes.

Enemy earrings that work against you:

- Earrings that hang from a wire hook are absolute "no-no's" for a professional image. Fine in your leisure time, these earrings announce a too-relaxed attitude for the workplace, regardless of what treasure may hang from the wire. The only exceptions: You work in an art gallery that sells a similar line of jewelry, or you are a sales representative who sells this kind of jewelry. In both cases, it is imperative that you wear fine, simple clothing and embody perfect grooming.

■ No long dangles — especially earrings that come to the shoulder — for a businesslike image. If you work in the beauty or fashion-related industry, high-class dangles may be okay. But tread carefully to maximize your professional status.

■ Many colored, enamel earrings do not look rich enough even for casual wear in the workplace. The colorful painted or enamel-on-metal earrings simply do not make an important statement for a woman aspiring to success.

■ Rhinestones and glittery evening earrings do not belong in the workplace on a daily basis.

Important necklaces — A necklace should add a flourish of power, silently fortifying your image in its entirety. It must look expensive and important to your overall outfit, or don't wear it! Make certain the metal finish coordinates with your other accessories. Example: A brushed-

FIG. 5:31 EMPOWERING NECKLACES

silver necklace does not mix with bright, high-sheen silver earrings. And bright gold earrings worn with a burnished (antique) gold-finished necklace or bracelet strike off-key chords. Pay

FIG. 5:32 EMPOWERING NECKLACES

attention to the coordination of all the details of your accessories (buttons on clothing, belt buckles, bracelets, etc.) to achieve that accomplished, exquisite, high-powered look.

FIG. 5:33 EMPOWERING NECKLACES

FIG. 5:34 EMPOWERING NECKLACES

Details surrounding the neckline area of an outfit make or break these pieces. For example: Small gems set in tiny bevels on thin chains are often lost in an outfit, making no worthwhile statement. On another ensemble, they might add just the right pizzazz.

FIG. 5:35 EMPOWERING NECKLACES

FIG. 5:36 EMPOWERING NECKLACES

Cuffing-Edge Bracelets

As with your other jewelry pieces, bangles and cuffs must coordinate with additional metals of your outfit.

Bracelet blunders produce sabotaging distractions in the workplace:

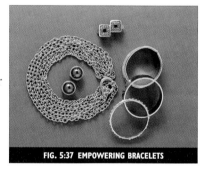

FIG. 5:37 EMPOWERING BRACELETS

FIG. 5:38 EMPOWERING BRACELETS

- Noisy bangles
- Too many bracelets worn at one time
- Cheap composites of metals that tarnish easily, even discoloring the skin.
- Glitzy, too-dressy styles
- Cloth styles (*especially* braided friendship bracelets)
- Whimsical or humorous styles (Unless they are in 14K gold or sterling silver; but be aware that howling coyotes do not speak the business language.)

Keep in mind that high-quality, pure metal (gold, at least 14K, and sterling silver) will look richer, making you appear more successful and capable.

Success-Cinching Belts

Belts should strike a profile for your profit just like your other accessories — even your casual belts. Add extra panache to casual clothing with distinctive belts. Make a point to own at least one high-quality *leather* belt in your best power-neutral color. Choose a few interesting — not bizarre — classy leather belts instead of owning an assortment of ordinary, inexpensive ones.

FIG. 5:39 EMPOWERING BELTS

Fashion rules no longer state that belts must coordinate with your shoes. Nonetheless, you will look well coordinated when *they* do. At the least, a belt must "make sense" with the shoes and the overall outfit. Be aware of the fabric mix when selecting your belts; leather and patent belts go with most fabrics. Suede belts require heavier fabrics to look appropriate. Example: A patent leather belt looks great with one-ply, sheer silks or cotton-piqué fabrics, while a suede belt works best with heavier four-ply silk, wool, knit, and jersey.

Elastic fabric belts — straw or plastic — do nothing to enhance your professionalism, your pocketbook, or your waistline. They only detract.

PRINCIPLE IV. IMPECCABLE SHOES = POWERFUL, PROFESSIONAL SMARTNESS

> *"Mom," asked the little girl, gazing up at her mother in awe, "When will I be old enough to wear the kind of shoes that kill you?"*
>
> – as reported by an anonymous shoe salesperson

Shoes tell secrets. Shrouded in the style and condition of your shoes, aspects of yourself are revealed. While they do not declare whether or not you are a "good person," impeccable or sullied shoes do announce:

FIG. 5:40 EMPOWERING BUSINESS CASUAL FOOTWEAR

- Your primary goals (if any)
- Whether you are lazy, indifferent, or diligent about the impact of your professional appearance
- Your tax bracket or socioeconomic group

Shoes are the foundation of your overall image. Empowered casual images require shoes that know how to walk toward profitable results. Smart shoes? Yes, indeed.

Take a look at these smart basics that will never steer you in the wrong direction in business.

Notice that the shoes shown above may not fit your version of what typifies a casual shoe. Remember, the competitive game of business demands that women stay on the dressier end of casual when they're dressing down. Your choice of footwear says a lot about your intention to succeed.

Here is a list of shoes that are considered "casual." Some shoe styles on this list are too casual — or are just not appropriate — for the workplace. Don't forget the range of the six classifications of casual attire. "Casual" does not imply one category. If you are confused, refer to Chapter 1.

FIG. 5:41 EMPOWERING BUSINESS CASUAL FOOTWEAR

Casual Shoes:

- Sandals (all varieties)
- Boots (even dressy versions make a relaxed statement)
- Shoes stitched in a contrasting color (white stitching around a shoe sole)
- Mules and all open-heeled shoes
  (Mules fabricated in dressy fabrics such as satin and silk are appropriate for evening wear or dressy daytime, but not for the workplace.)
- Flats
- Woven-leather footwear
- Lug-soled shoes (Regardless of how dressy the upper shoe may appear to you, if it has a rubber-like sole, it's casual. The more rugged the lug, the more outdoorsy the shoe.)

Whatever your style preference, stand firm on your goals for success by wearing only smart shoes. Protect their agile spirit and your investment with regular upkeep. Maintenance is critical for footwear. Casual shoes often require even more maintenance because they are worn more frequently and on rougher terrain.

Use cedar shoe trees inside your Business Casual shoes when you're not wearing them. Even if you don't live in a humid climate, leather and fabric footwear retains moisture. The toes will turn up unattractively in time without the regular use of shoe trees; they help to maintain the original shape. Cedar shoe trees are better than the plastic types because cedar removes moisture and odor. If you perspire heavily, sprinkle a small amount of foot powder in the bottom of the shoes before you put in the shoe trees. This lengthens the shoe's life span by helping to eliminate excess moisture that deteriorates the leather; foot powder also helps to eliminate odors.

PRINCIPLE V. STYLISH HAIR AND MAKEUP = A POWERFUL, PROFESSIONAL AURA

"Hairstyle is the final tip-off whether or not a woman really knows herself." — Hubert de Givenchy

As one of the first things people notice about you, your hair is a potent nonverbal communicator. Loudly broadcasting important details about you, your hairstyle reveals a great deal about your energy level and your emotional age. Are you stuck back in early adolescence? Does your hair project that you are prematurely old?

Vibrant hair amplifies a professional aura. Many women strive to dress professionally chic, investing money in quality clothing. Then they disempower their entire look with limp, tacky, outdated, style-less tresses. Split ends, home-color jobs, and faulty cuts make you and your clothing look second-rate or worse.

For ideas about current, businesslike hairdos, look at the national newscasters. Influenced by Hollywood fashions, the dramatic styles depicted in most magazines are not always appropriate for the workplace. Just as far-out, flamboyant runway fashions look silly for everyday streetwear, fashion magazines are not, as a rule, your best source for hairdos that exude professionalism.

Work with a hairdresser who understands your hair type: fine, extra-fine, coarse, naturally curly, etc. A versatile, talented stylist will talk intelligently with you about your hair type, its growth patterns, and what it will or will not do in relation to your face shape. Trust their expertise. You may get stretched out of your typical hair zone, but your personal and professional rewards will be worth it.

When making a big change in your hair, give yourself some time to adjust and get feedback from a variety of people who support your success. Even though they love you, your husband, boyfriend, or mother may not be your best critic. They are accustomed to seeing you through a certain filter. Hairstyle changes often unsettle those closest to us. They may need reassurance that just because you are now more beautiful and powerful, you are not leaving them.

Entire books have been written about face shapes and hairstyles; I will not attempt to address that subject in this book. I have worked with skillful hairdressers around the world, and I have collected a few helpful tips for certain types of hair:

- Fine hair must be layered to achieve volume; otherwise it lies flat against the head. Your face shape determines how much volume you need.

- Extra-fine tresses must not only be layered, but also notched cut — never blunt cut — to retain a distinct shape with its own volume. Some hairdressers call this notch cutting, point cutting.

- Coarse straight hair without body requires notch or point cutting too. With this hair type, a blunt cut looks ordinary, with no liveliness or style appeal.

- Unlike conditioner, which is applied to hair ends, styling products like gels or mousses must be applied only to the roots for these hair types. Comb the setting solution through to the ends only one time, and then blow dry. When a setting product is applied directly on the ends, the hair strands become heavy, dragging down the style. This drags you down too, making you look fatigued, with no sense of style.

The frame of your face, your hair color is critical in making a statement that supports your goals. For instance, gray hair can look lackluster, dulling your eyes and skin, producing a haggard and spiritless you.

With a stylish cut and the correct tone for your complexion, gray hair can be dynamic, projecting that you have wisdom and experience. Most women look more upbeat and powerful with blonde, red, or brunette hues rather than gray tones. (There are exceptions.)

If you choose to color your hair, consult a professional hairdresser. Once you do it, maintenance is imperative. Mismatched roots and severely damaged hair cast ugly shadows on you, diluting your professional demeanor. Successful women take the time to maintain their hair. Keep this in mind — a successful, rich appearance attracts greater success.

The halo of your overall image, healthy stylish hair is essential for casual empowerment. When dressing down for business, make doubly certain that your tresses are clean and styled. Remember, casual days are not licensed slob times, especially regarding your crowning glory.

Makeup Your Mind to Be Empowered.

Women who wear makeup earn incomes that are 20 to 30 percent higher! Well-done makeup, that is. More is not better. Even small amounts of blush, lipstick, and mascara add vitality to a face and pizzazz to a professional image. An appropriate use of cosmetics communicates that you care about yourself and that you give proper attention to detail. Heavy, overdone makeup points to low self-esteem or ignorance about what is appropriate. Ironically, a total lack of beauty aids sends the same message as overdoing it.

For the best advice regarding the use of makeup for your particular features, consult an authentic makeup artist who is not associated with a specific line of cosmetics. Salespeople in department stores have training with just a particular company, in most cases. While they may have some good suggestions, their main agenda is to sell, sell, sell you as many products as possible. (Of course, there are exceptions.)

Before we go into makeup application, let's talk briefly about one of the worst saboteurs for women: facial hair. Yes, we want glorious manes on our head, but on the face, hair is an offensive, negative distraction. Get rid of it! No excuses allowed. Whether it's a trace of a mustache, or under your chin, on your cheeks, your neck, your jawline, around your eyes (except for eyebrows), wherever — remove it. Methods for elimination vary. Some are permanent; others require consistent maintenance. Whether you prefer waxing, electrolysis, or other methods for your skin type, maintain a hairless face for ultimate professionalism. As women have more birthdays and their hormones change, a funny thing happens: While hair on the head may start to thin and eyebrows may require less tweezing, hair begins to appear all over the face and neck. Nose hair may even require more frequent trimming than your bangs! No, it's not fair, but actually it is just a minor problem. Aside from being distracting and unattractive, facial hair ages you unnecessarily.

There are no ugly women, only lazy ones.

— Helena Rubenstein

Makeup Guidelines for the Professional Woman:

WOMEN WHO WEAR
MAKEUP HAVE
20 TO 30%
HIGHER INCOMES!

■ **Foundation:** Match your foundation to your face, not the skin on your neck or your hand. Custom-blended varieties work best. *Prescriptives* offers an excellent custom-blend foundaton. Because it is mixed by hand at the cosmetic counter, your skin tone can be matched exactly. Your skin's moisture needs are also addressed with the *Prescriptives* formula. Apply foundation evenly all over your face, including your eyelids. Use a large fluffy brush (preferably mink), dust with matching translucent powder, or a powder slightly darker, to set the foundation. Don't use baby powder or talc unless you want to resemble a ghost. If you have clear skin, a moisturizer and bronzing powder may be all you need in the warmer months.

■ **Eyebrows:** Eyebrows frame your most precious art: your eyes, the windows to your spirit. Don't forget them! A rich eyebrow is well defined, without stray hairs. For a natural look, either dye them regularly or fill them in with a matte powdered eye shadow. Use a matte (flat-toned) eye shadow only on the brows; not even a smidgen of sparkle is allowed. Use an eyebrow brush with stiff, coarse hairs that are tapered, to fill in your eyebrows with eye shadow. When carefully done, this look is softer and more believable than the harsh lines or feathering of an eyebrow pencil.

■ **Eye Shadow:** Avoid frosty eye shadows in the workplace. If you're over 29, avoid them completely. (Frosted eye shadows age you by highlighting fine lines.) Be light-handed with color other than neutrals around the eyes for a professional image. Pinks can make you look as if you have been crying or suffering from allergies, particularly under fluorescent lights. Bright blues and purples look especially bawdy in fluorescent lighting — which most offices have. Use an eye shadow base (yes, on top of your foundation) on your eyelids before applying eye shadow for long-lasting wear.

■ **Eyelashes:** Curl them to open up your eye area. (Tweezerman makes an excellent curler; eyelashes do not stick to it.) Waterproof mascara stays on longer, smudges less, and endures watery eyes from allergies, re-wetting drops for contact lenses, or tears, without running or blurring your vision.

- **Eyeliner**: Your eye shape and eye size determine the placement and heaviness of eyeliner. Here is a lining technique that enhances all eye shapes: Lift your upper lashes and use a black, soft pencil to line the inside rim from corner to corner. This opens up the eye; your eye looks lined, but you do not see any obvious liner. If your eyes are sensitive to touch, you may have to train your eye to allow you to line this inner rim. But the effect is worth the effort!

- **Lips**: Line your lips with a lip pencil that is color-coordinated to your lipstick. Fill in your lips with pencil. Apply lipstick. Blot the lipstick, then outline your lips with pencil again for long-wearing color and lip definition. Avoid lip gloss for the workplace. If you insist, just touch the center of your lower lip with gloss and your entire mouth will shine.

- **Blush**: Correct placement of blush depends on your face shape. This rule of thumb applies to most face shapes: Look straight into the mirror, place your blush brush on your cheekbone, or just below, at the point that is in line with the center of your eyeball. Brush back toward your ear, following the line of your cheekbone. Don't leave a definite line. Blend your blush with a fluffy powder brush.

  To contour heavy cheeks, use a light taupe eye shadow under the cheekbone. A flat-edged brush works best for contouring. Suck in your cheeks (make a fish mouth) to apply the contour shadow. Start at the ear (that little center part) and brush downward toward your lips, following the line made when your cheeks are sucked in. Apply blush to cheekbone as described above. Then, blend the blush line and the contour line, using a fluffy powder brush. You might need to retouch your colored blush after this last blending.

- **Brushes**: The main hint when using cosmetic brushes or other applicators is this: The point on your face or eye that you first touch — with any brush containing blush or eye shadow — will retain the most color.

For instance, if you want more eye shadow color deposited on your outer eyelid, start there with your brush and spread the color inward. If you want more color concentrated on your inner eye area, start there with your brush and apply the eye shadow outward. Always use high-quality cosmetic brushes. Wash them regularly; bacteria builds up in brushes, causing you unnecessary pimples.

PRINCIPLE VI. PERFECT FIT = CONFIDENT, COMFORTABLE PROFESSIONALISM

> *"Style is a magic wand, and turns everything to gold that it touches."* — Logan Pearsall Smith

Correct fit is critical to your comfort and overall image. Unfortunately, many women spend big bucks on their professional clothing and then do not take that essential step to fine-tune each garment for a well-tailored fit.

A well-tailored jacket straightens your silhouette. Precise tailoring empowers, aligns, and slenderizes by concealing fat rolls, lumps, bumps, or other figure flaws. No puckering from the neck down allowed!

■ Puckers and rolls at the back of the neck and the area between the shoulder blades demand tailoring. That entire area should lie flat against the back. See Chapter 6, page 152 for an illustration of the correct fit.

■ Jackets that wrinkle or roll under the arm, at the waist, or the hip need to be adjusted for an impeccable fit. Button the jacket, even if you do not plan to wear it buttoned. Then sit down to see if the jacket pulls, puckers, or bulges anywhere. If the fit is correct, it will behave with no puckers. While still buttoned, check for rebellious wrinkles when you stand also. See Chapter 6, page 152 for an illustration of the correct fit.

WELL-TAILORED:

Correct fit is essential to comfort and the visual appeal of your overall image. A perfect fit exudes professionalism.

- Correct sleeve length marks a well-tailored jacket. Today's fashion requires sleeves to be worn a smidgen longer since the overall jacket cut is longer. If you are 5'4" and under, sleeve length is essential to your professional image, but you will almost always have to have yours shortened and tapered. If you are very tall, you have the reverse problem. You must buy high-quality garments only; sleeve lengths are cut longer. Nothing screams cheap like a too-short sleeve. For the well-tailored look, long sleeves should hit at the point where your upper thumb bone joins your wrist.

- Pleats tell the truth — they should lie flat against your lower abdomen and thighs. If not, you need a larger size. Spreading pleats visually enlarge your stomach and hip area. The waistline can be adjusted and the seat can be shaped on larger sizes. Do whatever it takes to make sure those pleats lie flat.

- Buttonholes that gape, barely holding the button on blouses or dresses, not only announce, but shout Cheap, Cheap, Cheap! Watch out for weight gain or shrinkage of fabrics from cleaning processes. Avoid the trap of thinking a different bra will handle it. If you are large-busted, avoid button-up-the-front blouses. Back buttons or pullover tops are for you.

Corporate Casual Chic

This section shows a wide range of empowering outfits that suit different fashion personalities and body types. Notice that none of these looks is dowdy or frumpy. Professional women today can dress with style and sex appeal, yet command respect. Be sure to also note the distinctions between the Corporate Casual Classics (Figures 5:42 and 5:43) and the Ultimate Power Casual variations (Figures 5:44 and 5:45). All of the Ultimate Power outfits have a dark jacket, or they are pantsuits, or they are a skirt worn with a jacket in a contrasting color. The Corporate Casual Classic outfits are powerful; but, on the whole, they make a less formal statement than the Ultimate Power ensembles.

FIG. 5:42 *corporate
casual classics*

Fashion is forever changing; such is the nature of that industry. Regardless of what styles are the rage at the moment, do not allow fashion whims to compromise your professionalism or to sabotage your potential or goals.

Let us now look to the wisdom of women who have blazed successful business trails. Some of them did so in times when it was not popular. Check out their attitudes about women and clothing.

"A fashionable woman wears clothes. The clothes don't wear her." – Mary Quant

"A completely indifferent attitude toward clothes in women seems to me to be an admission of inferiority, of perverseness, or a lack of realization of her place in the world as a woman. Or — what is even more hopeless and pathetic — it's an admission that she has given up, that she is beaten, and refuses longer to stand up to the world." – Hortense Odlum, President, Bonwit Teller - New York; 1939

"Clothes and courage have much to do with each other." – Sara Jeanette Duncan

"Elegance is not the prerogative of those who have just escaped from adolescence, but of those who have already taken possession of their future." – Gabrielle (Coco) Chanel

"Women who set a low value on themselves make life hard for all women." – Nellie McClung

"We all feel better when we take those few extra minutes to fix our hair and put on makeup, but what's more, we act different. Every actress knows the magic power of props and costumes to create special moods both onstage and off. None of us can be expected to perform every minute of our lives. But a lot of us might tap into the power, excitement, and glory of Real Life more frequently if we cast ourselves as the leading ladies in our own lives." – Sarah Ban Breathnach, *Simple Abundance*

You can have it all. Now more than ever, women are balancing families and careers. Use your image as a power tool to speed up your arrival and to increase your enjoyment of the journey. **Today — not tomorrow — dress for the job and the life you most desire.**

"Business
is a combination
between
war and sport."

— André Maurois

Empowering
Business Casual Essentials
for Men

Fighting wars and playing sports require strategies and the "right" gear. Uniforms — the style and color — distinguish whose side you're on in combat zones and sports arenas. In war, rank is also denoted in the uniform with epaulets, medals, or insignia. Although it's less obvious, business wear also follows the military model. In most cases, executives are easily distinguished from their subordinates by the formality of their attire, even when they are dressed casually.

Competitive negotiations are common in business. This is true even if you eschew the win/lose aspect of war and sports and ascribe to the millennium style of business — win/win. A less warlike attitude toward business does not mean that you cast aside your professionalism. As long as our free enterprise system continues, competitive products and services will exist. To survive and, better yet, to get ahead, you need a jump start that sets you apart from inferior commodities.

Just as a product's packaging often determines its marketability and success, your image serves as your packaging in the marketplace. Sharp attire stamps your demeanor and overall visual image with power and confidence, giving you a competitive edge. This is especially important when you dress down. Business Casual attire draws significantly from the traditional professional dress paradigm. When one strays from this model with too-relaxed apparel, demise enters like a cancer silently growing in your psyche and career. Remember, in the definition of Business Casual, personal power and professionalism are *never* sacrificed.

What components constitute "sharp" Business Casual attire?

Jackets:

Some things never change...

> *"A man with a good coat upon his back meets with a better reception than he who has a bad one."* – Samuel Johnson, as quoted in James Boswell's *Life of Samuel Johnson,* 1763

In most business settings, sport coats are appropriate on casual days. If not, they are easily removed. A great jacket will never let you down. If it's noteworthy, it will always add an air of power and authority to you. What constitutes greatness in a suit jacket or sport coat? Follow these pointers to hit the bull's-eye for a jacketed business image that attracts more success to you:

Fabric — high quality and natural. 100% fine wool tops the quality fabric list. How can you distinguish poor grades from fine? Easy — do the Touch Test. Fine natural fabrics — especially wool — feel good to the touch. If it scratches or feels rough to your fingertips, it does not qualify as "fine."

Lightweight tropical wool plays and works year-round in warm climates. Blends should be all-natural materials, such as wool and silk or silk and linen. Avoid polyester as if your very *life* depends upon it. (It does.)

Color — dark in tone. Navy and black are your most versatile choices for a jacket. Is there really anything else to express ultimate power? Take-you-around-the-world hues, both mix well with khaki, gray, brown, taupe, charcoal, and brighter colors — anything but each other.

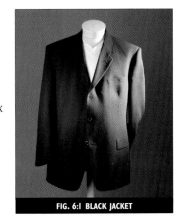

FIG. 6:1 BLACK JACKET

FIG. 6:2 NAVY JACKET

Lighter-toned jackets are not as versatile for business as black or navy, but they can look appropriate in the spring and summer or in tropical climates year-round. Still, there's no garment that powers up a man like a dark jacket!

FIG. 6:3 DARK JACKETS COORDINATE WELL WITH MANY HUES

Style — You choose: blazer type, double-breasted, single-breasted (includes one, two, three, or four button models). Traditional blazer cuts are generally shorter in length than other sport-coat styles.

Jacket types follow the same pattern as standard suit styles. Three models head the list: Classic American, Updated American, and the Classic European cut, which includes both the British and Italian styles. Classic American jackets are conservative in nature with no exceptional shaping characteristics. They feature a straight, untapered waistline, have no vertical darts, and do not emphasize the shoulders with extended shoulder pads. If used at all, their shoulder pads are small and soft — a more relaxed look. This jacket cut sports a single center vent in the back and is typical of the off-the-rack styles found at Brooks Brothers.

The Updated American version showcases a bit more style and shape and is manufactured by a wide range of designers around the world. This style sports a slightly tapered waist, some vertical seams to render shape, lightly padded shoulders, and a single center vent. Ralph Lauren's traditional suiting epitomizes the *Updated American* model.

FIG. 6:4 *front and back views of the Classic American jacket*

The American styles are generally cut a little shorter in overall length than the European cuts. The Classic American style shown in Figure 6:4 is longer than most traditional American styles. The cut shown here typifies the styling of the Hugo Boss line — longer and fuller.

Classic European styles attract the more daring, sophisticated guys (or those who aspire to be). This cut features a tapered waist, squared shoulders (usually extended), and high arm-holes. Classic British cuts generally have single or double vents in the back. In general, Italian styles have no vents, and they have the highest-cut armholes, the most tapered waist, and the most extended shoulders of any jacket style.

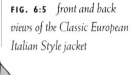

FIG. 6:5 *front and back views of the Classic European Italian Style jacket*

FIG. 6:6 *front and back views of the Classic European British Style jacket*

Two-button, three-button, and four-button styles all fall within these three cuts. Four buttons, and more look best on taller, leaner physiques — 6' 1" or over and slen-der. Double-breasted styles add breadth to the chest area. They are dressier and more formal and must be buttoned — *always*. Absolutely *no* exceptions — not even with jeans.

Try on a variety of styles. Using a three-way mirror, check out all angles. Observe how the lines work with your body. To check fit and silhouette, button the jacket: the top button on a two-but-ton, the middle button on a three-button, all the buttons on a double-breasted. Notice which styles rev your engine. You will feel more pow-erful, and you will look more powerful, if you wear the style that works best for you.

FIG. 6:7 SPORT COAT W/METAL BUTTONS

Buttons — Metal buttons dress down a jacket. Even though they are not ultracasual, gold and silver buttons on a jacket always mean that it is a true sport coat, not a suit jacket. Color-matched buttons mark a dressier jacket, a sport coat, or a suit jacket. It's not as tricky as it sounds; it's a matter of preference.

Both styles can be worn as a separate jacket to make a dressy statement, depending on what other garments they are paired with. Each jacket type may be worn with jeans (falling into the Smart Casual category). When worn with dress slacks, both belong in the Dressy Casual and Business Casual classifications of dress-down attire.

FIG. 6:8 SPORT COAT W/BUTTONS THAT MATCH FABRIC

FIG. 6:9 well-tailored jacket falls straight with no wrinkling at waist or hipline

Well-Tailored — Correct fit is essential to the comfort and the visual appeal of a jacketed physique. A well-tailored jacket straightens your silhouette. This trick emphasizes the all-powerful vertical aspect of a man's nature. Precise tailoring empowers, aligns, and slenderizes by concealing flaws in your physique.

No puckering from the neck down allowed! Puckering may work for kisses but it smacks of a cheap, ill-fitting garment in a sport coat. If you're buying off-the-rack jackets or suits, look at these three areas for a well-tailored jacket that empowers you:

■ Puckers and rolls at the shoulders, back of the neck, and the area between the shoulder blades demand tailoring. That entire area should lie flat against the back.

FIG. 6:10 well-tailored jacket lies flat at the neck and upper vertebrae

■ Jackets that wrinkle or roll at the waist or hip need to be adjusted for an impeccable fit. Button the jacket (top button on a two-button model, middle button on a three-

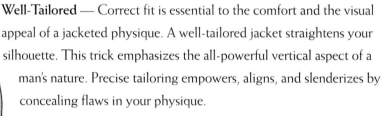

button style, and all buttons on a double-breasted jacket), and check front and back views for wrinkles or rolls at the waist or hip area. Then sit down to see if the jacket pulls, puckers, bulges anywhere. If the fit is correct, it will behave with no puckers.

■ The right sleeve length marks a well-tailored jacket. Today's fashion requires sleeves to be worn slightly longer since the overall jacket cut is longer now. Sleeves should fall just *below* the point where the thumb joins the hand to the wrist. To look up to date, jacket sleeves should allow one-quarter inch of the dress-shirt cuff to show (one-half inch at the most).

Jacket FAQs:

What suit fabrics allow me to wear my suit jacket as a separate sport coat too? Study the fabrics to the right to understand this subtle difference. Most men's stores stock a greater number of suits made in fabrics strictly for suits in their off-the-rack inventory; in most cases, they have fewer suits made in fabrics where the suit jacket can also be worn as a sport coat.

FIG. 6:12 FABRICS FOR SUITS ONLY

Figure 6:12 shows fabrics for suits only, never for separate sport jackets. For example: pin stripes, chalk stripes, light-weight poplins, serges, ottomans, seersuckers, and some glen plaids.

FIG. 6:13 DUAL-PURPOSE FABRICS

Figure 6:13 shows dual-purpose fabrics — for traditional suits, but also for sport coats. For example: solid-color fabrics (especially garbardines), micro-checks, windowpane checks, houndstooth, herringbone, and nail-head patterns.

To Vent or Not to Vent?

Vents are a matter of jacket design as discussed in the style section (see pages 150 – 151). Like pleats, vents should lie flat.

Vents are more of an issue if you carry extra weight in your rear. The single back vent is often said to be the answer for a large back end. I disagree. If the jacket is improperly fitted, too small, or cut too short so that the vent hits high on the hipline, another problem arises. A backside can actually kick out the center vent, drawing attention to this area even more, especially when you are walking (movement, in general) and viewed from behind.

The best jacket for a backside that carries extra weight is the side-vented style. You may need to enlist the services of a good tailor to give you the needed room around the hips and still make the shoulders and neck of the jacket fit correctly. Custom-made jackets can also fix this problem. Work only with a reputable tailor or get a "Made-to-Measure" jacket (or suit) offered in fine clothing stores.

Side vents can be easily closed, changing the jacket into a no-vent style. But don't do this, if you need any extra ease around the hips or thighs.

To button or not to button? Except for double-breasted models, sport coats can be worn open for informal wear. Double-breasted jackets must always be buttoned, even when worn with jeans, corduroys, or other casual garments.

FIG. 6:14 *jacket with no vents*

FIG. 6:15 *jacket with side vents*

FIG. 6:16 *jacket with center vent*

When you give a presentation, or whenever you need to create a more formal appearance while dressed casually, follow these Button Guidelines:

Button Guidelines for Jackets

- **Two-button jackets** — Button the top button only.

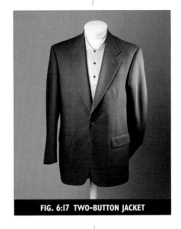

FIG. 6:17 TWO-BUTTON JACKET

FIG. 6:18 THREE-BUTTON JACKET

- **Three-button jacket**
  — Button the middle button only

- **Four-button jackets** — Button only the top three buttons, leaving the fourth unbuttoned.

FIG. 6:19 FOUR-BUTTON JACKET

FIG. 6:20 DOUBLE-BREASTED JACKET

- **Double-breasted jacket** — Button all the buttons, all the time.

Can jacket style make me seem taller and thinner? Always work toward the inverted triangle or V-shape to achieve a taller, thinner silhouette. This means selecting a jacket that has these two features:

1. Square shoulders (the pads extend beyond your natural shoulder line)
2. A tapered waist

Slight-in-stature guys (those 5' 7" and under) should avoid jackets with exaggerated shoulders; this look creates a horizontal line at your neck, which makes you appear shorter. On the other hand, the wimpy, soft-shouldered jackets often slope downward at the shoulders. That also takes inches off your height. A strong, square shoulder style works best for you.

**FIG. 6:21 TWO-BUTTON JACKET —
THE MOST SLIMMING SHAPE**

Which style has the most slenderizing effect? The two-button jacket (buttoned) is the most slimming because of the natural V-shape the lapel forms as it comes together with the button. The three-button model can also be slimming if the lapels naturally flow or taper down to the top button, forming the V-shape. Four-button jackets work best on tall, lean frames.

Can shorter men wear double-breasted fashions? Yes! In the past, only taller men were advised to wear the dashing double-breasted jacket. Clearly, this guidance is out-of-date. When impeccably fitted (especially with a semi-tapered waist), a double-breasted style pumps up the slight in stature — especially when worn with other fashionable, appealing garments and shoes. A double-breasted jacket requires cuffed pants, unless you are wearing jeans. The shorter man should opt for a 1¼" cuff.

PANTS:

"Show me a man with both feet on the ground and I'll show you a man who can't put his pants on." – Arthur K. Watson

Styles — For serious business wear, your best bet is a classic trouser that is pleated and cuffed. Flat-front pants with no pleats or darts make a more casual statement than pleated varieties. Not pocket-friendly, the flat-front models reveal keys, money, hands, or whatever else you're carrying or hiding. Choose the flat-front style only if you are lean.

Zanella offers the most impressive, comprehensive line of dress trousers in the world. Italian made, their line includes trousers that accomodate varying body types and style preferences.

FIG. 6:22 CLASSIC TROUSER PLEATED AND CUFFED

Cuffs? Yes, go for cuffs on your dress trousers for an updated look. Only out-of-sync men and ten-year-old boys wear non-cuffed dress slacks. Currently styles have at least 1¼" cuffs. If you are 6' and over, you have a choice of a 1¼" or a 1½" cuff — a matter of personal preference. Larger cuffs, such as 1¾", are for the fashion forward, avant-garde-type guys. Some tailors recommend the larger cuffs. But to play it safe in the game of business, opt for the 1½" or 1¼" cuffs.

Breaks? Today's vogue requires at least a medium break in the hem. At the minimum, the bottom of the cuff should come just below the line where the heel joins the leather body of the shoe. A longer break, a deeper fold on the front of the shoe, falls farther down onto the back heel — almost to the bottom. If you are 5' 8" tall or under, choose the medium break for your trousers. The longer one will drape too much, visually dragging your height down.

Fit — Pleats should lie flat against your lower abdomen and thighs. If not, you need a larger size. Spreading pleats visually enlarge your stomach and hip area. The waist can be adjusted and the seat can be shaped on larger sizes. Do whatever it takes to make sure those pleats lie flat.

Pant Fabrics: No fabric tops fine wool for a dress trouser. When they are in impeccable condition (clean and pressed), fine wool trousers always make an in-charge, authoritative, success-oriented statement. Lightweight tropical wool is comfortable even in warm climates in the summer because wool's natural fibers breathe.

FIG. 6:23 WOOL TROUSERS THAT WIN IN THE GAME OF BUSINESS

Cotton is an excellent natural fabric, but it conveys a more casual attitude than wool. Khakis and other cotton pants must be pressed and crisp to exude professionalism.

FIG. 6:24 FLAT-FRONT KHAKI PANTS — MORE CASUAL

FIG. 6:25 PLEATED KHAKI PANTS — LESS CASUAL

Linen works in some businesses for spring and summer trousers. Linen wrinkles. *"But they're wrinkles with snob appeal,"* says Chuck Haidet, one of the owners of Keepers, a men's fine-clothing store in Austin, Texas. Linen is found most often in high-class leisure apparel.

Depending upon what shirt or jacket linen trousers are paired with, the nonverbal communication can say dressy casual summer wear, resort apparel, or country club chic.

FIG. 6:26 LINEN TROUSERS FOR DRESS-DOWN PANACHE

Corduroy is a casual fabric for fall and winter wear. To be sure you won't be ribbed for wearing them inappropriately, remember the corduroy commandment: The wider the wales, the dressier the corduroy. Wide-waled cotton cords will make you look larger. Narrow wales are more casual, but they are more slenderizing. A new breed of corduroy, the microfibers, have ultrasmall wales. Because of their fabrication, they have a dressier feel than the traditional cotton cords shown here in Figure 6:27.

FIG. 6:27 NARROW-WALE TROUSERS

Avoid **shiny** polyester pants as if they carried a contagious, debilitating disease. They do. It's called Cheapitis. Polyester pants with a high-sheen finish can make you appear untrustworthy — like the used-car-salesman type. They belong in nightclubs, not in the workplace.

Even regular polyester pants do not drape well on your body. One hundred percent polyester fabrics are hot (temperature wise). The fibers do not breathe; they trap in your body heat and cause perspiration. If you love polyester because it does not wrinkle, then at least buy a blend of fabrics that includes some natural fibers like wool, silk, or cotton. Some of the new microfiber fabrics (a blend of polyester and wool) are excellent for travel because they do not wrinkle. And they do breathe a little, depending on the percentage of wool. However, if you are warm-natured, even the microfibers will make you feel warmer. Besides, wrinkle-free should not be your primary goal when acquiring pants that win in the game of business.

Shirts:

"Taste cannot be controlled by law." — Thomas Jefferson

When you dress down, your shirt takes center stage. Without a jacket as your business armor, your shirt reveals the level of professionalism you bring to your work environment. The quality and condition of your shirt disclose whether or not you have good taste, whether you look successful, how well you take care of your belongings, and who you really are.

CONSIDER THESE FACTORS BEFORE YOU CHOOSE A SHIRT STYLE:

- How do you want others to perceive you, *before* you say a word?

- What nonverbal statement do you *want* to make?

- What statement should you make to be aligned with your goals?

Positive aspects of any shirt style work only when the fabric (cotton, silk, or linen) is of top quality and the shirt is clean and pressed.

Shirt Styles and Their Statements

FIG. 6:28 TRADITIONAL BUTTON-DOWN COLLARED SHIRT

■ **The Button-Down** — The traditional version.

Pros: It's tidy. The collar stays put, and the ends don't curl up or flap in the wind. Mr. All-American, this shirt announces that you are conventional (no renegade here). It inspires trust from other conventional folks. Informal in nature, it pairs well with other classic casual wear, such as khakis, corduroys, or jeans.

Cons: As its button-down-the-hatches name implies, it makes a conservative statement, hinting that the wearer might be closed-minded or even lazy (no collar stays required). Some consider the button-down "dowdy," and without flair. It says that your preferred sandbox of life is not much farther than your own backyard. Check, stripe, and plaid button-down shirts are in the Sporty Casual category. Give up even the solid-color varieties, if you want to play in the international business arena.

Common Mistakes:

1. Wearing a button-down collared shirt with a double-breasted jacket marks you as an oxymoron with no fashion sense. Wearing these two garments together is like trying to be blond and brunet at the same time.

2. Wearing an unbuttoned button-down collar is a no-no. It doesn't create a positive casual image. Instead, it suggests that you need someone to dress you, or that you might not follow through on important tasks.

Regions of Popularity:
   – The United States (New England, the Midwest, and the South)
   – Great Britain
   – Ireland
   – Australia

FIG. 6:29 EUROPEAN BUTTON-DOWN SHIRT

■ **The European Button-Down** — Sometimes referred to as the Euro-collar. This shirt is a different breed from the traditional button-down. The collar comes to a distinct point, buttoning in the center of the collar, a good inch above the point.

Pros: The points behave, staying down just the way they are supposed to. When you wear a tie, the collar sides hug it nicely, delivering an orderly appearance. This collar suggests that the wearer has a progressive outlook. It's sleek, sharp, and cosmopolitan.

Cons: Fashion illiterates may think you are wearing the traditional button-down, missing the Euro-collar nuance.

Common Mistake: Never unbutton the points or you will be flapping in the wind.

Regions of Popularity:
- European-designed, this shirt is popular all over Europe, especially in Switzerland.
- United States — major metropolitan areas, particularly New York, Chicago, Los Angeles, San Francisco.
- Australia — especially Sydney and Melbourne
- Canada — Toronto, Montreal, and Vancouver

FIG. 6:30 CLASSIC POINT COLLAR — CASUAL

■ **The Classic Point Collar** — Not the scissor-point collar, just the standard point. The casual versions are designed to be worn with or without a tie.

Pros: Urban in nature, it's sophisticated. This shirt has style and is globally accepted as classic. Even without a tie, when buttoned up to the neck, it projects an air of formality, which increases any authoritative stance. It looks striking with pleated dress trousers as well as jeans.

Cons: The classic point-collar shirt requires a lot of maintenance; it demands to be sent out to a professional laundry or dry cleaner. If the shirt has no collar stays and is not properly pressed, the collar ends can flip up awkwardly, or just droop in Milquetoast fashion. If the shirt comes with collar stays, they must be taken out before cleaning and then put back in before wearing — a time-intensive duty.

Common Mistakes:

1. Though the casual variety is designed as an informal shirt (tie optional), some of the collars are not meant to be worn open. In that case, you must button up all the way to the neck for this shirt to look empowering.

2. Wearing the collar-stay variety without any collar stays makes you look sloppy and disorganized. If you hate dealing with collar stays, look for point-collar shirts that have the hidden snaps that hold the points in place.

Regions of Popularity:
Countries around the world respect this shirt style. It's worn globally.

■ **The Banded-Collar Shirt**

FIG. 6:31 BANDED-COLLAR SHIRT

Pros: No fuss, no muss — it stays in place. It's hip. Slightly clerical in style, wearing it can inspire trust. In the right fabric, it is elegant, especially in white worn with a dark jacket. The collar can be worn unbuttoned or closed. When you are giving a presentation, or you want to appear sophisticated with authoritative panache, button up. The banded-collar shirt conveys that you can think outside the box, but you are not subversive.

Cons: Raised-collared sorts may generate "priestly" comments. For long-neck guys, raised bands are flattering. If you have a short neck, forget the stand-up bands altogether. If you have a broad neck, sizing may be a problem because the band may fit too tightly. This shirt has peaks and valleys of popularity in high-fashion circles, but it remains classic. When it is not the fashion rage, it is hard to find in stores. Some shirtmakers offer this collar as a special-order or custom-made item.

Common Mistakes: The neck must fit correctly. If it's too big, a giant chasm between the collar and skin makes your neck look wimpy. On the other hand, chokes are for engines, not shirts. Folds of skin overlapping a too-tight collar are unsightly, making even the observer feel uncomfortable.

Regions of Popularity: Metropolitan areas around the world.

FIG. 6:32 COLLARED-KNIT SHIRT

■ **The Collared Knit Shirt** — Cotton is the most common fabric here, but it is also made in wool, silk, and blends of all three.

Pros: It's comfortable and relaxed, and the cotton ones are washable. This kind of shirt wears well under a suit jacket or sport coat, especially for travel. A long-sleeve collared knit shirt makes a Smart Casual outfit with dress trousers.

Cons: Cotton knit shirts have short life spans even when dry cleaned. The fabric starts to get nappy or ball up in six to eight months (if not before).

Regions of Popularity: Cities throughout the United States, Canada, South America, Europe, Australia, and Asia.

■ **Ultimatum Collars** — These shirts always demand a tie! Don't even think of wearing spread-collar or tab-collar shirts for casual wear, untied or tie-less.

Designed as a dress shirt, the **spread-collar shirt** looks awkward without a tie. There is too much space there because of the spread. This collar works best for men who are slightly thin in the neck (but not too thin), because it gives the illusion of width by spreading the distance between points. Designed on Savile Row in London, this shirt is commonly worn with a suit. It plays well in the casual arena when worn with a sport coat, dress trousers, and a tie (Dressy Casual).

FIG. 6:33 SPREAD COLLAR DRESS SHIRT

ALWAYS WORN WITH A TIE!

This collar can communicate stuffiness and no imagination. Because of the spread, it calls for a larger tie knot than has been in vogue recently.

Tab Collars demand a tie; otherwise, the tab shows. This shirt was designed to keep the collar closely around the tie knot — especially the small knot — and to keep the tie in place.

This collar hints that you are meticulous, precise, and detail-oriented. It looks best with a suit or dressy sport jacket.

FIG. 6:34 TAB COLLAR

ALWAYS WORN WITH A TIE!

Shirt FAQs:

What about cotton T-shirts? Can I wear them for a casual dress code or dress-down days? Cotton T-shirts do not communicate serious business. They tee off many bosses, especially when you wear them with jeans and sneakers. To command respect, a T-shirt can be worn for business only if it meets these four criteria:

1. The shirt is plain, with no sports logo or emblems.
2. The shirt is medium- or heavyweight cotton — not threadbare thin.
3. The shirt is pressed — not wrinkled.
4. The T-shirt is worn with a sport coat and you don't remove the jacket.

Solid-color T-shirts made in fabrics such as silk, linen, and wool speak a more sophisticated language for the workplace than cotton ones do. T-shirts in these fabrics can be worn without a jacket and still look smart. But even these should not be worn for business if they fit too tightly, nor should they be worn in the workplace if they are too thin, revealing chest hair or muscles.

What about pullovers like turtlenecks, mock turtlenecks, and crew-necks? Sophisticated and comfortable, a top-quality dressy pullover (not a sweatshirt!) is a great alternative to the conventional shirt. Just how sophisticated depends upon the fabric and the quality of the shirt as a whole. These shirts wear well with all pant types: dress trousers, jeans, corduroys, or khakis. Tucked in or worn out, they look cool with a jacket.

FIG. 6:35 EMPOWERING PULLOVER SHIRTS

Should I wear an undershirt? What kind? Personal preference is the answer here; there is no right or wrong. If your shirt is so thin it needs an undershirt, do not wear it — toss it! Many guys who perspire heavily prefer an undershirt; it helps protect the top shirt. And in colder climates, an undershirt is warmer.

A statement is made when the neck of your undershirt shows around the collar area of your buttoned-up shirt or knit shirt: 1) It signifies a preference for the "preppy" look; 2) It announces that you are the very conservative sort — possibly old-fashioned in some way. (I am not saying that these are bad messages to send.)

Sending a Mr. Gigolo message, a tank-type undershirt worn with the top shirt unbuttoned far enough to reveal your skin and your undershirt is a major error in the workplace.

SHOES:

"Luck is being ready for the chance." – J. Frank Dobie

Whatever your business, the only guarantee life offers is change — and not the pocket variety, either. Are you ready to take advantage of all the opportunities that come your way? Even at unexpected times? Are your shoes walking you toward success, or are you buying and wearing the sort of shoes that run in the opposite direction?

Shoes — the foundation of your image — are tattletales. Whether casual or dressy, your shoes advertise these details about you:

- Your primary goals (if any)
- Whether you are lazy, indifferent, or diligent regarding the impact of your professional image
- What tax bracket you're in or the economic group you aspire to
- How you manage details, especially items requiring maintenance

With this in mind, the main question becomes what shoes fortify the message you want to project and are appropriate as casual wear in the business arena. First, let's look at the five key features that make a shoe casual:

■ Dress shoes differ from casual shoes in that they typically tie. (Think lace-ups.) Casual footwear does not tie. (Think slip-ons.)
Dressy Exceptions: Satin, silk, or patent-leather slip-on tuxedo shoes or opera pumps.
Casual Deviations: Some casual footgear ties, such as lace-up ankle boots, or suede wingtips with a lug sole and white stitching.

■ Shoes stitched in a contrasting color (white stitching around a dark shoe sole) are always casual.

■ Woven-leather footwear is always casual. In lizard, it's sharpshooting Smart Casual, but it is still not considered a dress shoe (like for power business attire or formal wear).

■ Lug-soled shoes. Regardless of how dressy the upper shoe may appear to you, if it has a soft sole, it's casual. The more rugged the lug, the more outdoorsy the shoe.

■ Shoes made from suede or buckskin and shoes with matte-leather finishes.

SURE-BET DRESS-DOWN SHOES

■ If you cannot polish them

■ If you cannot apply a high sheen

■ If you cannot buff them

This list clarifies exactly what marks a shoe as casual. I do not mean that all the casual shoe types listed above are appropriate for the workplace. For instance, there are dressy slip-on shoes that you *can* polish — even to a high sheen. Those are far more empowering when they're worn with wool trousers as part of a Dressy Casual outfit than a lug-sole shoe would be. Dressy slip-on shoes are more empowering when they're worn with jeans as part of a Smart Casual outfit than a deck shoe with white stitching would be.

FIG. 6:36 EMPOWERING BUSINESS CASUAL FOOTWEAR

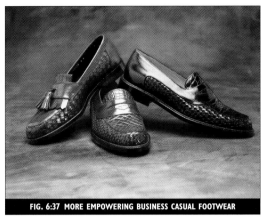

FIG. 6:37 MORE EMPOWERING BUSINESS CASUAL FOOTWEAR

To exude casual power, smart shoes are a necessity. Your shoe choice must complement your outfit as a whole. Take a look at these shoes that point you in the direction of success.

SOCKS:

"Everybody is ignorant, only on different subjects."
— Will Rogers

Socks? Yes, wear them. Naked feet are not prepared to play on business turf. Your color sense and pattern-recognition talents surface when you select socks. Some people have it naturally, some don't. Choosing appropriate socks is a skill worth learning.

To demonstrate you have sock savvy, follow these tips:

■ **Sock color should be in the same tone as your pants.** Example: Light-colored pants, such as khaki, look best with light-colored socks, even when worn with dark shoes.

FIG. 6:38 LINEN PANTS W/BEIGE SOCKS AND BLACK SLIP-ON SHOES

FIG. 6:39 PATTERNED SOCKS HAVE NAVY AND OLIVE TONES

■ **For multicolored, patterned socks, look to the other colors in your outfit to find the right blend.**

■ **Buy tall socks.** Bare skin is exposed when you cross your legs, if your socks are too short! Little old men wear brief socks.

■ **The heavier the sock, the more casual it is.** The shoe should get more substantial (larger, bulkier) in accordance with the weight of the sock. Tuxedo socks are extra sheer; do not wear them as casual.

■ **Always wearing solid-colored socks marks you as an ultraconservative type,** possibly timid, or with no imagination.

■ **Your socks should not be the first thing people notice about you.** Wearing bold, wild-patterned, weird-colored socks that scream for attention portrays you as a schizophrenic "wannabe."

■ **Shop for socks in men's fine clothing stores.** Find a salesperson who obviously has good taste and sock savvy — look at how they are dressed. Ask sock-it-to-'em questions. Unless there is a sale or a special store event, most well-trained salespeople are happy to share their expertise.

BELTS:

"Self-denial is not a virtue, it is only the effect of prudence on rascality." – George Bernard Shaw

Are you cheating yourself with a wimpy, worn-out cheap belt? So you have a great jacket, you've shelled out big bucks for your shirt, your trousers, and shoes — and now you're worried about breaking the bank? Are you thinking no one will notice the cheap belt if the other garments are of high quality? Beware! That sort of thinking zaps you straight into the middle of the casualty zone.

To exude casual power, wear high-quality all-leather belts that cinch your success. Here are some basic rules for your belts.

■ **The more metal on a belt, the more casual it is.** (Visualize large Western-wear buckles.)

■ **Woven-leather belts are casual. Matte-finished leathers are casual.** Shiny finishes always make a dressier statement, so they're a must when you're going for the Dressy Casual look.

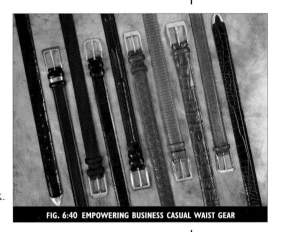

FIG. 6:40 EMPOWERING BUSINESS CASUAL WAIST GEAR

■ **Elastic belts with leather fronts are *not* empowering.** Yes, they are casual — and they have zero class, zero panache, zero income-gathering skill. They have no value and no place — not even on the golf course — in your success-oriented wardrobe.

■ **Belts should be in the same color tone and finish (matte or shiny) as your shoes.**

Jewelry:

"Have more than thou showest, speak less than thou knowest."
– Shakespeare, "King Lear"

Success leaves visual clues. It does. It should. Nonetheless, the rule for businessmen and their jewelry reads like this: Easy does it. Over-doing jewelry in a business setting works against you by inspiring suspicion and distrust. In this unnamed crime, you are the prime suspect. Follow these jewelry suggestions to exude professionalism and command respect.

■ **Two rings (maximum) for business wear.** Choose authentic, high-quality metal and stones for a professional image that attracts gold-lined success.

■ **No visible neck chains** or other neck ornaments if you mean serious business.

■ **One bracelet cuff** (simple design) in 14K gold or sterling silver is acceptable.

■ **Earrings?** If you have to ask, the answer is no.

■ **Cufflinks are the ultraprofessional business accessory.** French-cuff shirts are made for suits and more formal wear. Do not wear them with casual attire, even with a sport coat and tie. Always avoid those clip-on "faux cufflinks."

■ **Metal watches are the most empowering for business wear.** Numerous styles of empowering metal watches are available. Avoid watches with diamonds until you own the company, you're public — listed on a certified stock exchange, and the stock is soaring. You are sure to get ahead with a watch made of gold, stainless steel, or a combination of gold and silver. Stainless steel is the sturdiest (highest performance rating) metal if you prefer a silver-toned watch.

– Pocket watches are an excellent alternative to wrist timepieces. They convey sophistication and individualism.

– Waterproof diving watches or gadgety watches are not impressive in the workplace, unless your job is related to one of those industries. These watches say that sports are your main priority, not your job or the business at hand.

HAIR AND GROOMING:

> *"He needed a haircut — especially at the nape of*
> *the neck — in the worst way."* — J.D. Salinger

A man's hairstyle points to his attitudes about himself and how he thinks others see him. A man's ambition is gauged by his daily grooming habits, which are revealed, in part, by how he keeps his hair. Is his hair generally unkempt or is it almost always immaculate? An updated style, periodic haircuts, and routine shampoos are essential to the businessman who wants to succeed.

There is not just one particular hairstyle for men that is the most businesslike. Those guys who have worn the left-sided part for forty years may be surprised, but there are many other hairdos that work well for business. The trend for the '90s and beyond is away from the precise part. Even if that style looks great on you, I encourage you to loosen up the part — at least a little. A precise part in a man's hair suggests that he is old-fashioned and ultraconservative, and may not be up-to-date with what is going on now, especially regarding technology.

A man's hair type (coarse, fine, straight, curly, etc.) and his face shape determine his best look. Consult a reputable hairdresser or stylist to identify your most flattering hairstyle. The most important element of a businesslike hairdo is that the hair is clean and neat. It does not have to be an ultraconservative style, but it should not be a totally outrageous one either. Those styles belong on the stage or in nightclubs.

Hair is not everything; some of the most powerful, handsome men I know are bald. For those of you who are bald or whose hair is thin on top, grooming your head and side hair is still important. If your hair is just about gone on the top, my advice to you is to embrace being bald, get hair transplants, or buy an exceptional-quality toupee. But don't comb long side hairs over your balding pate. You're not fooling anyone! This look detracts from your professionalism and ruins your chances for having a powerful image. It immediately signals that you're having problems accepting your baldness; you're advertising your weak link. Instead, focus on highlighting your eyes — maybe even darkening your eyebrows. Bald men can command as much respect, look as powerful, and be just as attractive as men with full heads of hair — especially when they are well-dressed and carry themselves with confidence.

Don't stop with only a haircut. Other areas need attention too! Unruly eyebrows and neck hair are big distractions. Most hairdressers will also trim eyebrows and neck hair. Ask your stylist for that service. Should you have a *lot* of neck hair, shave it yourself on a regular basis or see a barber weekly.

Many men today color their hair and dye their eyebrows to enhance their looks. Eyebrows are especially important. For many of my male clients, I recommend regular tinting of the eyebrows. Strong eyebrows can add power to the face. Just don't overdo a dark color and end up with a Frankenstein image.

Speaking of overdoing, use a light touch with fragrances and scented shaving lotions in the workplace. If you can easily smell the scent you just applied, it's too much! In addition to strong smells being annoying, many people are allergic to fragrances.

The question of whether or not facial hair is appropriate for business always arises in my workshops and consultations. There are some men that a moustache, a beard, or a goatee suits well, but those men are rare (*especially* goatees). I have found that if you look back to the period of time when a man grew his moustache, beard, or goatee, there was something going on in his life that was making him uncomfortable or that he wanted to hide from others. The reason could be simple; he may have wanted to cover up acne scars or what he perceived was a weak chin. Even though all forms of facial hair have their moments of popularity, if you peek into your past, your real reasons for nurturing facial hair may surprise you.

Facial hair hides your face; consequently, it generates distrust from others, at least on the subconscious level. If you prefer to have a beard, moustache, or goatee, just remember that you may have to work harder to inspire trust. This is especially important if you are in sales. It is less true for professors and psychiatrists or for other professions that have a bearded stereotype.

Excellent grooming is the key to facial hair that does not detract from your professionalism. Beards and moustaches must be thick — if not, don't even try to grow either one. They must be trimmed on a regular basis for you to win in the game of business. You may have to accelerate your trimming schedule in the spring and summer; hair grows faster in the warmer months. Read my lips: A moustache must not drape over your mouth if you want to have any professional clout. Keep it trimmed!

A casual day is no excuse for not shaving. Remember, power up when you dress down. Being well shaven and looking well groomed are major components of a commanding presence when you're wearing casual clothing.

The following pages contain a panorama of casual outfits appropriate for winning the game of business, including ensembles for different fashion personalities, tastes, and body types. Be sure to note the distinctions between the Corporate Casual Classics (Figure 6:41) and the Ultimate Power Casual variations (Figures 6:42 and 6:43). All of the Ultimate Power outfits have a dark jacket, or they are suits worn with a dressy shirt (no tie) or a dressy sweater. The Corporate Casual Classic outfits are powerful; but, on the whole, they make a less formal statement than the Ultimate Power ensembles.

FIG. 6:41 *corporate casual classics*

FIG. 6:42 *ultimate power casual variations*

FIG. 6:43 *more ultimate power casual variations*

Take a look at what these wise guys had to say:

Men and Clothing

"Clothes make the man. Naked people have little or no influence on society." – Mark Twain

"When a man is once in fashion, all he does is right." – Lord Chesterfield

"The way to expand our lives is to model the lives of those people who are already succeeding." – Tony Robbins, *Awaken the Giant Within*

"We first make our habits, and then our habits make us." – John Dryden

"If we all did the things we are capable of doing, we would literally astound ourselves." – Thomas A. Edison

"I believe that life is constantly testing us for our level of commitment, and life's greatest rewards are reserved for those who demonstrate a never-ending commitment to act until they achieve." – Tony Robbins

"Each impression you make will — temporarily, at least — be your last. So make it strong." – Harry Beckwith, *Selling The Invisible*

Fashion is forever changing; such is the nature of the industry. It is important to look current, but not to be victimized by fashion fads. Be loyal to your body type and to your professional and personal goals — at all times.

Remember: You can have whatever you want if you dress the part. Don't settle for an ordinary life with an ordinary image. Be extraordinary! Increase your personal horsepower and accelerate your success. **Today, not tomorrow, dress for the job and the life you desire most.**

"Uncertainty kills business."

— Michael Edwards

Certainty Leads to
Casual Empowerment

Certainty leads to success. Uncertainty wastes time and scatters energy. While life provides indisputable aspects of uncertainty, looking doubtful and confused in the workplace is deadly.

In this chapter we discover how to look casually empowered, no matter what the workplace dress code may be, even if you are required to wear a uniform. The last segment of this chapter deals with the hesitant hazards of packing for business travel.

DRESS-DOWN DILEMMA #1:

When no company guidelines exist.

Excessively casual attire will show up in this scenario. It's guaranteed. When there are no rules, people tend to create their own, and usually far below the ideal or even the norm. To shine professionally and personally, do not join the lowest common denominator. Be your own boss and establish some clear professional-dress rules for yourself — self-imposed, self-generated guidelines that accelerate you along the "Super-Success Expressway."

Remember the taunting tricks of McSly if you are teased or ridiculed for dressing well when the majority does not. By adhering to high empowerment standards, you silently hold up a disquieting mirror for others. This activates *their* mind chatter. Be friendly, but take no abuse and do not give in to a lower standard of dress. In time, you may notice others joining you in presenting a consistent professional image.

Encourage management to set some basic guidelines, if that is appropriate without jeopardizing your job. Give your manager a copy of this book! Why? Because ambiguity is fertile ground for the personal saboteur to raise its ugly head. Saboteurs thrive in groups as well as individually. Dress code parameters handed down from the "powers that be" leave little room for a treasonous saboteur.

DRESS-DOWN DILEMMA #2:

When precise company guidelines do exist.

If your workplace has specific codes for professional dress, follow them to the letter — and farther — especially if you like your job, want to keep it, want a raise, want a promotion, or want a good or better recommendation when you leave. You can still dress with individual expression under the strictest of codes. Then dress any way you want to in your off time.

These codes were NOT set down by your parents. Rebellious employees ask to be treated like adolescents, with required policing and monitoring. Get over the urge to get strokes from negative attention. If you are receiving a paycheck, it is time for you to act like a mature adult and get with the program. If you don't, only you will lose in the end.

Some managers are sticklers for the rules and actually measure skirt lengths, etc. If you find yourself in this situation, remove yourself from scrutiny and possible criticism by following the codes. Be impeccable. Be the best you can be (do it for yourself). You will win and gain respect.

According to human resource experts, your boss can legally ask you to dress professionally, in compliance with that company's codes. It is legal to send you home to change or to fire you for not complying — even in California, where the laws often favor employees. What a boss cannot do is to ask an employee to buy expensive designer clothing. This is illegal.

DRESS-DOWN DILEMMA #3:

When company uniforms are required.

Many companies have uniforms or a version of a uniform for dress-down days. The dilemma: How can you stand out in the crowd when you are forced to wear exactly what all the other employees wear?

For starters, usually several garments are an optional addition to the basic outfit. This is particularly true for banks on Casual Friday and for telecommunication companies that embrace across-the-board casual dress codes.

> **Casual Uniform Example — basic outfit for men and women**: Khaki pants, collared knit shirt with the company logo on the right side, white sneakers, and white socks.

> **These optional pieces are usually offered**: Long-sleeve cardigan, varying tops or shirts, like a long-sleeve regular shirt/blouse or a turtleneck top in the specified color.

If you have a choice, opt to wear the long-sleeve garments. You will look more professional than the short-sleeve folks. A cardigan or vest worn with either suggested top will have a jacket effect, lending an air of power and authority to your casual image. If you don't work outdoors, ask if you can wear hard-sole shoes instead of sneakers. Keep your socks or hosiery thin and light-colored for the khaki pants even when wearing brown or black leather shoes. Wear an all-leather belt, even if you are wearing sneakers.

If you have no options to the uniform, follow these guidelines to shine with professionalism and stand out in the crowd:

STAND OUT IN THE CROWD; EXUDE CASUAL UNIFORM POWER

- Each garment must exude crisp cleanness and be pressed well. Khakis should be starched and ironed or professionally dry cleaned.

- Wear the assigned shirt, including the knit top, buttoned up all the way to the neck. Women can wear an appropriate necklace if desired. Male or female, if you wear the collar open, you will diminish your professionalism and authority.

- An all-leather belt is mandatory. Do not wear any form of elastic belt.

- Your sneakers must be impeccably clean — like new! This includes your shoelaces.

- Your hair must be clean, dry, and styled — preferably a great cut with flair. No wet hair, no wash-and-wear hair.

- Your nails must be clean and manicured. (This includes you guys, too.)

- To exude casual power, women must wear makeup and high-quality professional-type earrings.

- Stand tall and hold your shoulders back. Exude confidence with excellent posture!

Southwest Airlines sets a good example for casual uniforms. The flight attendants look sharp and pulled together, not sloppy or lazy. Uniforms are never an excuse to slide by with a less-than-professional image.

BUSINESS TRAVEL PACKING GUIDELINES:

Kick confusion out of your closet. Pack for your business trips, certain of exuding top-shelf professionalism each day you are away. Refer to the "Capsule Wardrobe Plan" defined in Chapter 4. These magical garments will take you anywhere in the world in first-class fashion. Always survey the weather for your destination before you pack.

Check out cities via the Internet or the newspaper, or phone ahead to inquire.

Packing Guidelines for Men:

For a four-day conference (**Business Casual** attire suggested): Be comfortable, but look powerful and successful when you travel and arrive. You may have valuable networking opportunities en route, perhaps a once-in-a-lifetime occurrence.

Get in the fast lane. On the plane or in the car: Wear a long-sleeve knit shirt with color-coordinated dress trousers, khakis, or corduroys; a sport coat (or a suit jacket that can double as such); dressy leather slip-on shoes; and a high-quality leather belt.

Pack These Items:

FIG. 7:1 NAVY SUIT
W/KNIT SHIRT

■ **One solid black or navy suit.** If you are wearing the suit jacket as a sport coat on the plane, just pack the matching suit pants. Pack one additional sport coat that coordinates with your suit pants and your second pair of trousers (the ones you are wearing on the plane). If you are wearing the suit with the knit shirt for travel (as shown in Figure 7:1), be sure to pack an additional pair of dress trousers that coordinates with the suit jacket. Or you can wear one suit and pack a second suit that mixes well with the pieces of the first suit.

■ **Four to five shirts** that can be mixed and matched with your suit jacket, your sport coat, and either pair of trousers (or the second suit). Vary your shirt fabrics, colors, and collars for diversity in your image. This is especially important when you are wearing the same jacket several times. Choose shirts that do not require a tie to look immaculate.

■ **Four pairs of socks,** coordinated to your trouser and your suit-pant colors.

■ **Four pairs of underwear** and your preferred sleepwear.

■ **Toiletries** — Shaving needs, toothbrush/toothpaste, deodorant, medications, hair products, etc.

■ **If desired, pack these items as extras:**
  – Additional pair of shoes that coordinates with your other garments.
  – Extra belt that corresponds with the above pieces.
  – Another pair of trousers that coordinates with your jackets and shirts.
  – Workout clothing, including sneakers.

■ **Other possible extras:**
  – Cold-weather gear: overcoat, gloves, wool scarf.
  – Rainy weather gear: umbrella, raincoat.

FIG. 7:2 DRESS TROUSER AND SHIRT — SUIT JACKET OR SPORT COAT COULD ALSO BE WORN W/THIS OUTFIT

From the basic list and what you wear on the plane, you have varying options of outfits to wear at the conference. Figures 7:2, 7:3, and 7:4 show three of the possible combinations — and even more variations considering the jackets.

FIG. 7:3 DRESS TROUSER W/KNIT SHIRT AND SPORT COAT — NAVY SUIT JACKET COULD ALSO BE WORN W/THIS OUTFIT

FIG. 7:4 NAVY SUIT AND RED POINT-COLLAR SHIRT — ALTERNATE SPORT COAT COULD ALSO BE WORN W/THIS OUTFIT

Considerations: Depending upon how the conference is scheduled, i.e., daytime only with no semiformal dinners, one jacket may be adequate. By following the above plan, you have a clean shirt to wear every day. The pullover can be worn more than once, if necessary. Be *sure* to hang up the dress trousers at the end of each day so the wrinkles can fall out and they'll be ready to go again on an alternate day.

Avoid traveling with high-maintenance fabrics like linen. This is not a license to wear cheap polyester. Wool and cotton travel well if folded properly. Read the section on folding that follows the women's section (page 191).

Packing Guidelines for Women:

For a four-day conference (Business Casual attire suggested): Be comfortable, but look powerful and successful when you travel and arrive. Valuable networking opportunities may arise en route — possibly even one of those once-in-a-lifetime happenings.

Get in the fast lane. On the plane or in the car: Wear a long skirt or pants coordinated to a solid-colored jacket and a long-sleeve knit top or blouse. (If you remove your jacket, you still look empowered when you wear a long-sleeve top.) Also wear all-leather pumps (closed toe and heel), a high-quality leather belt, and the jewelry of your choice — professional-looking earrings are a must.

FIG. 7:5 BLACK SUIT W/GRAY TURTLENECK

Women's clothing offers greater variety than menswear does. For this reason, it is more difficult to formulate an exact packing prescription. Here are some suggestions for basics from which you can create many ensembles. Use these criteria to choose garments that fit you and that travel well.

Pack These Items:

■ **One solid black or navy pantsuit.** You might be wearing the suit (at least the jacket) on the plane, as in Figure 7:5.

■ **One additional jacket,** in a color and/or pattern that coordinates with your navy or black suit pants. This jacket can be sportier and more casual than your suit jacket, and it can be in a totally different color.

■ **One extra skirt or pants** that coordinate with both jackets.

■ **Three tops or blouses** that can be mixed and matched with both jackets, the skirt, and the pants. Vary your fabrics and necklines to achieve different looks.

■ **Shoes, one additional pair** that coordinates with the other garments you are taking.

■ **Four pairs of hosiery,** coordinated to your skirt and pant colors. Three pairs might be enough if you rinse them out at night. (Use the shampoo provided by the hotel as laundry soap for your hose.) Always take an extra pair of hosiery for emergencies. Don't assume you can buy your favorite brand there.

■ **Jewelry** that coordinates with each outfit. Pack several pairs of earrings. When you are wearing the same jacket, vary the earrings and other jewelry from the last wearing. For example: Wear gold accessories with your long-cut black jacket and black pants one day; silver worn with the same garments changes the look and is more casual. The outfit looks even more different with a blouse change when you change the

jewelry. Don't worry about changing watches. Always power up with
basic metal.

■ **Four pairs of underwear**, bras, panties, and preferred **sleepwear.**
If you need a particular bra for any of the tops or blouses, be certain to
pack it. Slips? Only necessary with see-through fabrics. Otherwise, do
not wear them.

■ **Toiletries** — Makeup, toothbrush/toothpaste, deodorant, hair products, hair appliances (hairdryer, hot rollers, curling iron), medications,
razor, perfume, skin-care products, etc. (Use the hair conditioner provided by the hotel as shaving lotion when you shave your legs.)

■ Pack these items as extras:
  – Extra coordinating belts.
  – Another skirt or other pants that coordinate with one or
    both jackets.
  – Scarves.
  – Tops and jewelry that can change your basic pieces into
    appropriate dinner attire (not formal dinner attire).
  – Workout clothing, including sneakers.

■ **Other possible extras:**
  – Cold-weather gear: coat, gloves, hat, wool scarf.
  – Rainy weather gear: umbrella, raincoat.

From the basic list and what you wear on the plane, you have varying options of outfits to wear at the conference. Figures 7:6, 7:7, and 7:8 show three of the possible combinations — and even more variations considering the jackets.

FIG. 7:6 PANTS W/
LONG-SLEEVE KNIT BLOUSE —
ADD RED OR BLACK JACKET
FOR VARIATION

FIG. 7:7 THE SKIRT W/
ADDITIONAL JACKET

FIG. 7:8 BLACK PANTS W/
PATTERNED BLOUSE —
ADD RED OR BLACK JACKET
FOR VARIATION

Considerations: Women should take two jackets for a three- or four-day conference. Remember, women are more easily disempowered with casual dress than men are.

Be *sure* to hang up your garments at the end of each day so the wrinkles can fall out and they'll be ready to go again on an alternate day. If you prefer skirts over pants, take all skirts. Pants or a long skirt can be more comfortable and wrinkle less than short skirts when you will be sitting for long periods.

Avoid traveling with high-maintenance fabrics like linen. (This is not a license to wear cheap polyester). Wool and cotton generally travel well if folded properly.

Tips on How to Pack:

Okay, we know where you are going and what you are taking. How do we get it all in one carry-on bag? It's possible with a medium-sized roll bag. If you have a lot of extras, you may need one additional small bag. If you prefer a hanging bag, you can still glean many packing tricks from the information below.

Before placing anything in the suitcase, get *everything* ready for packing. If you're not already dressed, separate all your clothing pieces, shoes, and other accessories that you will wear on the plane or in the car. Then place all other items (see the previous checklist) in a convenient packing area. Check off each item as you prepare it for packing.

■ Place shoes in a shoe bag or wrap them in cloth or plastic.

■ Place all easy-to-wrinkle shirts, blouses, or tops in plastic dry-cleaner bags — one garment per bag.

For example: Hold a shirt by its collar (with the neck button and top three buttons buttoned) and pull the plastic bag over the top to cover the entire shirt. With your other hand, grasp the collar that is now covered with the plastic. Straighten the shirt and lay it (plastic encased, front side down) on a flat surface. To begin the folding process, take a shoulder and sleeve and fold it back on one side, folding toward the back center of the shirt. Fold the other shoulder and sleeve in the same way; place it carefully as that sleeve will overlap the other sleeve. Make sure the sleeves are not twisted. Now fold up the bottom of the shirt (4" to 6"). Then fold again, taking the bottom fold and placing it even with top edge of the collar. Turn over the shirt and it should look professionally folded, although encased in plastic. The dry-cleaner bag folded between the layers of the garment cuts down on wrinkling, if you take care to fold the item properly.

You may use tissue paper instead of plastic bags to decrease the wrinkle factor. If you are the meticulous type, you can even stuff the sleeves with tissue paper. But this will cause the folded shirt to take up a lot more room in your suitcase. One of my clients thought he was being clever by using newspapers, but he ended up with newsprint all over his white shirt. I perfer to use plastic dry-cleaner bags over tissue paper because they are easy to use and I always have some extras in my closet.

- Place your folded, plastic-encased garments on top of the heavier items already packed. This does not include jackets. They go in this section of the rolling bag last.

Do not fold pants, skirts, or trousers yet. They get handled differently.

- Fold all the other items on the list.

- Place the heavier items in the main compartment of your suitcase (a mid-size roll bag). Place them in the order shown below.

PACK ITEMS IN THIS ORDER

- Place heavier, flatter items on the bottom.

- Shoes, cosmetic bag, or shaving kit can go in as a center divider for folded items. (If you use a cosmetic bag, make sure all products are sealed well and wrapped in plastic.)

- Place lighter items, especially those wrapped in plastic, on top of the other items.

- Do not roll belts. Place them around the edges of the suitcase. Tuck any delicate buckles into underwear or another fabric item.

- Fold extra jackets in plastic and lay them across the top as shown. Fold over the shoulder end of the jackets. Do not fold up the bottom edges; those creases do not come out easily.

■ Put your jackets in dry-cleaner bags, following the same procedure as described on page 191. Then fold each jacket in half (lengthwise) with the lapels or collar facing out. Lay the jacket across the top of your already packed items. Fold the jacket over at the shoulder end, not the hem end. Hem-edge creases do no come out easily. Because jacket shoulders are padded, fold that end over making certain that the jacket hem is even with the edge of the suitcase (Figure 7:9). Fold any extra plastic over the top.

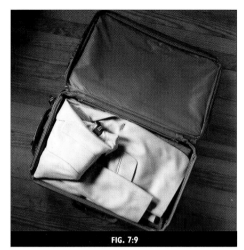

FIG. 7:9

You may add other jackets by alternating the shoulder ends, as shown in Figure 7:10. (Unfortunately, we could not show any garments wrapped in plastic bags because the plastic reflected too much light for

FIG. 7:10

the photographer to get a readable shot.)

■ Zip up this section.

■ If a heavy topcoat is necessary, don't pack it. Carry it on the plane with you; you may need it when you arrive. Bulky garments like coats require too much room to pack. Turn the coat inside out to fold it up. This reduces wear and tear and potential soiling while it is stored in an overhead compartment or in the trunk of a car.

FIG. 7:11

■ Now we are ready to pack trousers and skirts. Place each garment in a plastic bag. Placing trousers in a plastic bag is a little trickier, especially if they are lined. The same procedure applies; encase the entire garment inside the plastic bag. Fold the trousers or pants in half, bringing the seams together to keep the creases in place. Then arrange them in the hanging or "suiter" part of your bag, as shown in Figure 7:11. Remember you have removed all hangers from this area.

The waist end of pants should lie flat against the edge of the suitcase. Let the pant leg overlap the side. You will fold these up, laying them straight across the top, as you alternate the layers of pants. This process puts only a slight wrinkle around the knee area; it usually falls out easily after the pant has been hanging for about one hour.

■ Place pants and skirts flat, in alternating fashion, in the top section of the suitcase as shown in Figure 7:12.

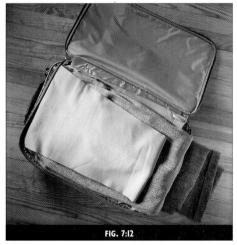

FIG. 7:12

■ Skirts, short and long, should be folded back at each side to fit the width of the bag. Short skirts usually fit the length of the bag. If not, make the skirt shorter by folding from the waist area (once it is inside the plastic bag); do not fold the hem edge. Long skirts should be doubled in length. If there are any wrinkles at all, this technique places a slight crease mid-skirt, as if you had been sitting in it. This wrinkle also falls out easily after the skirt has been hanging overnight.

■ **Zip up this section.** (Figure 7:13 shows the pant leg turned back in this section. We only did that so that you could see the layers of pants and skirts folded in the suiter compartment.) **You are ready to go as soon as you check the list. You may need to put extras in another *small* carryon.**

FIG. 7:13

■ **Hang up all your garments as soon as you arrive.** In a few hours, any wrinkles should fall out. If not, you can turn on the hot water in the bathroom shower for a few minutes, then hang any wrinkled garments in the steamy bathroom and the wrinkles will disappear. Allow some cool-down time before you wear them. Fabrics wrinkle worse when damp or warm, even immediately after ironing.

■ **If you prefer a hanging bag:** Use plastic dry-cleaner bags around each garment. They help the wrinkle factor. Leave jackets unbuttoned, or only button the top button before you place them in the plastic bag. Be sure to straighten the sleeves and the entire garment after you hang it in the bag.

"Fashion is made
to become
unfashionable."

— Coco Chanel

8

Acquiring
a Business Casual Wardrobe
on *Any* Budget

"How long will this be in?" is the primary question for a shopper con-
templating a hefty price tag. This is an important question considering
that the temperamental fashion trade thrives by changing styles repeatedly. New sales each season are the wheels that keep the entire industry
in motion. Designers, manufacturers, wholesalers, and retailers perpetu-
ate their businesses through seasonal products that are new and different from the previous season.

In the fashion world more than four seasons make up a year.
Instead of only four, there are seven. Wholesalers of the Apparel Marts
and World Trade Markets offer designers' wares at market times that are
months prior to the actual delivery time to retail stores. Purchasing
agents for stores buy their fall inventory at the spring markets and buy
their spring merchandise at the fall market. Depending upon the needs
of their clientele and their climate, retail buyers may or may not shop

all seven market periods. Most large department stores buy at least part of various designers' lines at each market.

Why is this information relevant and important to the ordinary shopper? If you want the créme-de-la-créme selection each season, your timing is crucial. Knowing when new shipments will arrive gives you a leg up on making prime selections. The retail fashion calendar notes these time ranges to receive merchandise:

SEVEN FASHION SEASONS — PRIME-TIME RETAIL ARRIVALS

1. Cruise apparel (mid-December to early January)

2. Early spring fashions (late January to early February)

3. Spring/summer styles (late February to mid-March or early April)

4. Transitional lines for early fall (mid- to late July)

5. Fall fashions (late August to early September)

6. Winter styles (September to early October)

7. Winter holiday lines (mid- to late October)

By using this same information, the bargain shopper can gauge the timing for price reductions. Most stores mark down merchandise after a couple of months, sometimes after only a few weeks, to make room for their new seasonal items. Prime bargain selections peak before a sale is advertised publicly. Preferred customers receive private invitations to shop the sales first; however, the stores are not usually closed to the public during this time. It's just a matter of timing to join in a bargain extravaganza.

Even when it's timely, shopping can be frustrating and overwhelming. With the jungle of inventories prevalent in most retail scenes, shoppers need machetes to cut their way through to the apparel that suits them best. Be wary of getting in the boxing ring with McSly when purchasing your clothing. The brain easily shuts down from sensory overload when it's confronted with numerous choices of varying designs, colors, fabrics, and styles. This debilitating condition interferes with your efficiency and clouds your judgment. Let's take a deeper look and find out if this common phenomenon has affected you. Keep in mind the experiences of your own shopping expeditions to answer the following questions.

When shopping for clothing, have you ever experienced any of these warning signs?

- Sudden feeling of total exhaustion, so that your arms and legs feel so heavy, it takes too much effort to move
- Yawning and drowsiness
- Headache
- Dizziness or a light-headed sensation
- Extreme thirst or dry mouth
- Eyes burning or feeling heavy-lidded
- Feeling disinterested or dazed
- Too tired or distracted to make a decision
- You purchase a garment that you do not really like just so you can go home

These symptoms are classic to *"Sensory Overload."* The human eye can only make so many distinctions at one time. When you are barraged with choices, it is common to experience one or more of the above. All nine are indications that your mind feels overwhelmed and is signaling you to take a break. Those who experience more than four of the symptoms at one time should steer clear of large department stores. Smaller boutiques that have fewer displays of inventory are the best choice for the sensory-sensitive.

Training your eye to seek out items you want to view closely reduces the chance of defeating your shopping efforts. A set of complex factors plays into the shopping process. Efficient shopping is a skill that can be learned. My workshops on how to shop effectively highlight eleven all-purpose Painless Shopping Strategies. Employing these strategies when you build an empowering Business Casual wardrobe ensures that your purchases will support your professional and personal success. When you go shopping, always keep in mind the nonverbal communication that you most want to project.

PART I – PAINLESS SHOPPING STRATEGIES

- Make a Plan
- Know Your Stores
- Know Your Finances
- Know Your Body Type
- Command Extraordinary Service
- Know Your Size Ranges
- Buy Quality
- Know Your Power Colors
- Time Your Shopping Trips
- Expect Alterations
- Think Capsule Wardrobe

Make a Plan

Have your agenda in hand. Know what items you are shopping for, instead of making haphazard purchases at random. Survey your closet first, making a list of your "needs." Then buy as your finances permit. Refer to the information on the Capsule Wardrobe Plan (Chapter 4) if you are unsure of what you should add next. Jot down what you lack while you are getting dressed every day. This way you are not standing in the store scratching your head, thinking *"Now what was it I needed to buy to create the empowering look I want?"*

Without a plan, it is extremely easy to get sidetracked and arrive back home with garments that do not really work for you. Clarity leads to power. Knowing exactly what you need or want to buy enables you to be an empowered shopper.

Know Your Stores

Decide ahead of time what specific store or shopping area you are going to. Main considerations should be: what designers or labels they carry in their inventory, their general price points, which charge cards they accept, their return policies, and their layaway policies (if any). If you have serious financial considerations, call ahead for this information.

Know Your Finances

Even if money is not an obstacle for you, it is best to look into your personal finance crystal ball *before* you go shopping. Know exactly how much cash you can spend and/or how much room remains on your credit cards. If you have only one specific credit card you wish to use, phone the stores to be certain they take that card before you waste your time shopping there, i.e., Neiman Marcus honors only their own card, American Express, and Diners Club; they do *not* accept MasterCard or Visa. Having this information before you even enter any store can take away much of the subconscious anxiety and pressure most people feel when shopping. Clarity leads to power; when you know exactly what you can spend, you are an empowered shopper.

Know Your Body Type

This is a major key to painless shopping. When you are familiar with the nuances of your body type and you know what styles are flattering to you, you can easily scan multiple racks of clothing for possibilities. By "know your body type," I mean that human beings are endowed with many different bone structures. (Your particular body "type" has nothing to do with how much you weigh.) Honestly evaluate your body and do so *without* judging your type as being good or bad. Unless you are a supermodel, most people require certain cuts and styles to highlight figure assets and to minimize problem areas.

Volumes are written on varying body structures and exactly what types of garments most flatter each type. I encourage you to read one of these books or hire a wardrobe professional, or just learn from trial and error. A full-length mirror is essential when looking for those all-important distinctions. Even small style changes or alterations make a huge difference in how clothing affects your silhouette. Make a concerted effort to learn these key features about *you*:

Vital Statistics for Female Body Types — *Know Your Body*

■ **Height** — This measurement is not as critical for women because their jackets are not sized in "long" or "extra-long" as men's jackets are. One of the more significant questions for women is *where* is your height? Are you long or short in your torso (the trunk of your body)? Are you longer or shorter in your legs?

If you are long in your torso in comparison to your height, you are long-waisted. Avoid clothing that makes your waist look even longer because this will make your legs appear short: i.e., dropped waist skirts or pants; tunic tops or long blouses (those not made to be tucked in) worn with full skirts or wide-leg pants. Also, avoid belts that are color coordinated to your upper-body clothing. For instance, if you were wearing gray pants with a black top, you would want to wear a gray belt to make your legs look longer. A black belt would lengthen your waist-line and make your legs look shorter.

If you are short in your torso, you are short-waisted. If your waist is not located just under your bottom rib, this can be an asset because your legs appear longer. Short-waisted women should avoid clothing or accessories that accent their midriff, like wide belts or clothing with pockets, buttons, or other ornamentation on your midriff and waist areas.

■ **Hipline** — The most important *unchangeable* body-type distinction for females. Are your hipbones set high, medium, or low?

> **High Hip** – Tends to have a little bit of a tummy regardless of weight. If you put on a few pounds, it shows up first in your front tummy area and your upper waist. Your buttocks are relatively flat, even if you are wide in the hips. In general, your buttocks are not extremely fleshy or protruding, but you have hipbones positioned just below your waist that can collect weight (often called love handles).
>
> **Do:** You look best in straight-lined clothing, not tight, just straight-lined. The waistband of your skirts and pants must have

---

> **RULE OF THUMB WHEN CLOTHING ALL BODY TYPES:**
>
> *Don't bring attention to the areas where you are short in comparison to your height. A perfectly proportioned bone structure is the illusion you want to create.*

absolutely no gathering — not even the tiniest bit. Pleats must be stitched down, or be long enough so they do not protrude with your tummy. Trouser pleats must point outward toward the pockets, not inward toward your stomach. Pants pockets set at an angle are the most slenderizing. High-rise pants and skirts work well for you.

Don't: Elastic waists are deadly! Any shirring or gathering around the waist area instantly adds 10 to 20 visual pounds. Avoid excessive fabric in the thigh area unless you are very tall. Also avoid pants cut long in the stride. Shun designs with drapes or details around the tummy area and avoid A-line skirts that have the inverted pleat in the center. Waist length or mid-abdomen length blouses, tops, and sweaters worn out (not tucked in) emphasize and exaggerate even the slightest tummy. Avoid these styles, unless you are quite thin.

Low Hip – Tends to be long-waisted, with a relatively flat stomach, and a small waist with larger buttocks, regardless of how much weight you carry.

Do: Elastic waists, gathering and pleating give you ease around the lower hip and thigh area without adding visual weight to your silhouette. Long jackets that come below your upper thigh area look terrific.

Don't: Don't expect skirts or pants to fit you both in the waist and in the hips without alterations. Alterations are essential for you. For garments to properly fit your hipline, the waist must be taken in because it will be too big. Avoid straight skirts that are too tight and pants that are cut short in the stride. Be careful of short jackets; they do not work for you if you carry extra weight. Also avoid mid-length jackets or blouses that end at the middle of your buttocks. Instead, choose styles that are either shorter (hitting on or just below your waist, well above where your buttocks begin) or styles that are longer, completely covering your hips.

■ **Neck** — Long or short? A long neck is an asset. Turtlenecks, mock turtles, mandarin collars, jewel necklines — all high necks — are flattering on you. If your neck is exceptionally long, these styles are best for you at all times; you should avoid V-necks, long necklaces, dangle earrings, or any lower neckline that adds more visual length to your neck area.

If you have a short neck, V-necks and open collars work best for you. Avoid all turtlenecks, plain round necklines, and choker necklaces.

Vital Statistics for Male Body Types — *Know Your Body*

■ **Height** — Every man should know his *real* height because it determines your jacket length.

- If you are 6' tall, you may need a Long (L) in a jacket (depends on your torso length).
- If you are 6'1" to 6'2", you definitely need a Long (L) in a jacket.
- If you are over 6'2" to 6'4", you require Extra Long (XL) in a jacket.
- If you are over 6'4", you need to shop in a tall man's shop (like Rochester Big and Tall).

Where is your main height? Torso? Legs?

- If you are long in your torso in comparison to your height, you are long-waisted. Avoid clothing that makes your legs appear short — i.e., dropped waist pants, trousers with lots of fabric in the thigh area, tunic shirts or shirts worn out (not tucked in).
- If you are short in your torso, you tend to be short-waisted. If your waist is not under your armpits, this can be an asset. Your legs will look longer. With this body type, wear dropped-waist pants or shirts not tucked in, *only* if you are tall.

■ **Weight** — Where do you carry your weight? Tummy? Rear?

- If you carry extra weight in your tummy, trouser pleats should go in the direction of the pockets, with pockets set at an angle to maximize the slenderizing effect. Pleats should be long enough so they do not protrude excessively with your tummy. Loosely fitted, straight-lined, untapered double-breasted jackets are a good option for you, if you are not short in stature. Avoid flat-front pants.

If you carry extra weight in your rear, vents on jackets present a problem. Read the vent section in Chapter 6 (page 154) for the details.

- **Waist** — Measure it around your real middle.
  - Waist measurement determines correct trouser size.
  - Add 1 inch to this measurement for your correct belt size (usually).

- **Neck** — Measure it around the Adam's apple, allowing one finger width of room.
  - Neck measurement determines your correct shirt size.
  - If you your neck is quite thin, avoid scissor-point or tab collars that create a pinched look at the neck. Go for a standard point collar or semi-spread.
  - If your neck is large, avoid *any* version of spread collars because they add visual width. Banded collars may propose a problem for you; be sure to buy them large enough so that your neck does not spill over the band when the collar is buttoned. The body of the shirt can be taken in to fit you properly, and sleeves can be shortened. But get the neck big enough! This is true for all shirt styles.

- **Expect Alterations**

Few people can buy clothing off the rack and wear it without getting alterations. If you fall into that category, you are indeed blessed. The rest of us must get alterations to achieve a custom-fitted look. Searching for garments that require no alterations causes frustration and wastes your valuable time.

While alterations take extra time and money, they are worth the effort. Garments that fit correctly are more comfortable, and they add an aura of excellence to your image. Correct sleeve length, proper hems look. A custom-fitted look is essential to exuding personal power and top-shelf professionalism.

■ Know Your Size Ranges

Honesty about your sizes aids you in shopping efficiently. Your correct size will vary according to the manufacturer or designer. I've shopped with women who bought garments ranging from a size 6 to a size 12 — all depending on the designer. Sizing for men does not vary that much.

Don't get hamstrung about the numbers. Sizes are just that — numbers. Get your ego out of the way. It's far better for a garment to fit well and be flattering than to cram yourself into a smaller size that is uncomfortable and looks too tight. Remember, no one else can see the size printed on the inside label. (Remove it, if it bothers you.)

■ Know Your Power Colors

Power colors are rich, deep shades of black, navy, brown, gray, green, red, or burgundy. Determine whether navy or black is the best neutral for your basic business garments. This reduces the number of shoe colors and accessories necessary to present yourself with empowered panache.

■ Timing

Allow yourself time to shop in a relaxed manner. The fewer pressing time concerns you have, the less likely you are to make shopping mistakes. Avoid shopping when you are hungry, thirsty, or emotionally or physically exhausted. Making bad purchases adds to your other problems. Go to the bathroom, feed yourself, hug a tree, see your therapist — do whatever it takes to be clearheaded when you make clothing purchases. Keep in mind the best timing for abundant inventories and dollar-saving sales.

■ Buy Quality

Know quality, and be a "quality connoisseur." Think in terms of Amortization, not Sticker Shock. High-caliber fabrics and well-made garments outwear cheaper versions. Always, always, always buy quality.

Recognizing quality clothing is a skill that can be learned. Just as one doesn't learn to speak French by studying German, understanding quality clothing requires exposure to high-caliber fabrics and well-constructed garments. Browse through several designer sections, such as Armani, Escada, Sonya Riekel, etc., for women, and Brionni, Zegna, Armani, etc., for men. Observe the detailing, the fine workmanship, and the quality fabrics. Literally touch and caress some of the fabrics to train your fingertips to make distinctions based on the feel of high-quality fabrics. Examine the excellent construction, looking at the seams, hem stitching, and linings.

Some items in a Couture department are not viable choices for a career wardrobe; they are exotic showpieces for a glamorous lifestyle or for the fashion runway. However, these departments are excellent classrooms to develop your skills in recognizing quality.

BRAND THIS LIST ON YOUR DOMINANT HAND — *the one that reaches for your wallet.*

QUALITY CHECKLIST

- Fabric
- Construction
- Hem
- Zippers
- Pleats and Vents
- Pattern Matching
- Pockets
- Buttons
- Linings

■ **Fabric** — Is it natural (wool, linen, silk, cotton) or is it a blend? If it's a blend, what is in it? Polyester is often listed in labels as acetate. The new microfibers are a blend of some natural fabrics, but the main yarn is polyester. High-quality goods are generally made of natural fabrics.

What type of finish is the fabric treated with, permanent press or soil-resistant? Fabric finishes may seem like a good idea, but they do not wear as well as untreated goods.

Polyester is hot! Trapping the body heat in, polyester allows for no breathing of your pores or the fabric. It causes perspiration, and it can increase body odor. The manufacturing process for polyester contributes enormously to global pollution problems.

■ **Construction** — Check the workmanship on the inside of the garment. The better the garment is made, the better it will wear and hold up to cleaning and your abuse. Look at the seams. How many stitches per inch? The more stitches per inch, the stronger the seam. The tension of the stitches needs to be tight, but not so tight that the seam puckers. In excellent construction, all seams lie flat, are straight, and have generous seam allowances and finished edges.

Check how the linings are sewn. They should not affect the drape of the exterior garment by causing wrinkling, pulling, or puckering. Make certain that linings are sewn well around armholes, shoulders, and hems. On long-sleeve garments, be sure to check sleeve hems for puckering or clutching the arm when you put on the garment.

■ **Hems** — Bad hems scream Cheap, Cheap, Cheap! Ideally, you should not be able to see the stitching on any hem. Sheer, transparent, or extremely delicate fabrics demand hand-rolled hems. If the garment you are considering passes all the other tests, the hem may be able to be redone. Main question: Is there enough length to re-hem without sacrificing the line of the garment or its flattering effect on you?

■ **Zippers** — Zippers should lie flat with no puckering, inside or out. Sometimes exposed zippers are fashionable, but in classic garments, zippers are covered with a placket. Check the stitching on the outside of the placket — it should be very neat. Zippers should be in the same color hue, an exact match of the garment fabric color. Zip up and down a couple of times to check for any snags or hesitations. If you fall in love with an item with a faulty zipper, check it out with an expert or walk away from it. (Be wary of a salesperson's advice that it is a simple procedure to put in another zipper.) Correction is often extremely difficult, if not impossible. Find out about the return policy of the store if you want to take the garment to a tailor or alterations expert.

■ **Linings** — Should always exactly match the garment fabric in color. Check suits to be sure that the skirt or trouser lining is the same fabric as the jacket lining. Acetate is a common lining fabric. Finer couture garments use silk, or silk taffeta if the garment needs a stiffer lining.

Patterned garments should have a lining that matches the dominant background color of the print. Jackets and full-length coats should be fully lined. High-quality garments are always fully lined, except for men's trousers. Fine wool drapes better if not lined all the way down the leg.

■ **Pleats and Vents** — Pleats should lie flat with no puckering or standing out from the garment. All the pleats on your trousers, slacks, or skirts must lie perfectly flat. If not, the garment is too small. Try the next size and tailor down in the areas that are too big. If the pleats still do not lie flat in a larger size, there is a design or construction flaw that is NOT correctable. This is true for back vents and pleats, as well.

■ **Patterned Fabrics** — Check the seams on prints, plaids, herringbones, checks, and stripes to make sure they match. They should come together perfectly at the shoulders, the sides, and the back seams. If they do not, quality is sorely lacking.

■ **Pockets** — Deep pockets — don't we all love deep pockets! Pockets should be roomy enough to fall deep inside the garment. Otherwise, they can show by creating ripples in the exterior fabric. Check the pockets for neat exterior stitching. Many high-quality tailored garments are designed with besom pockets. This style offers the flexibility of wearing the finished flap out or wearing it in for a cleaner simple look. Pockets will show through in light-colored fabrics if not lined properly.

■ **Buttons** — Bound buttonholes are the finest quality. The stitches should be close together, finished neatly with no loose-hanging threads. Test the alignment of the button with the buttonhole by actually buttoning the garment; it should line up perfectly without creating any pulling.

Couture designers often use plastic buttons on the inside of the garment to reinforce the outer button, helping it to stay securely stitched to the garment. For very delicate, flimsy fabrics, a high-end design has its buttons backed with muslin, just behind where the button is sewn on.

The stiffer muslin is then covered with matching fabric that helps to secure or reinforce the exterior button.

Don't let bad buttons stop you from buying an item that otherwise is great. Some of my best purchases went through a facelift with new, quality buttons. Fabulous buttons can upgrade a garment, but poor choices can ruin an otherwise wonderful garment. Warning: Changing buttons requires a good eye and good taste, and it can be time-consuming. If you're not well-versed in the art of button-sewing, have a tailor or a reputable dry cleaner do the job for you.

Think: Capsule Wardrobe

Chapter 4 devotes an entire section to the Capsule Wardrobe. This minimalist approach to dressing consists of a few essential garments as the heart of your business wardrobe. Purchase this core group before shopping for the extras. Simplifying the shopping process, the Capsule Wardrobe is a delight for the hurried shopper or for a tight budget.

Focus on one capsule at a time for painless shopping. When adding pieces to the capsule, keep in mind that all garments must work well together. Because of its pared-down nature, a Capsule Wardrobe that gets you ahead demands quality garments. Always, always, always buy quality over quantity.

Command Extraordinary Service

A terrific salesperson is a valuable ally for a pain-free shopping experience. You don't have to take all their opinions to heart; their primary job is to sell, sell, sell. But if you have a salesperson who has obvious good taste (look at how they dress), they are more likely to tell you the truth.

The main advantage to cultivating a strong relationship with a salesperson is the service you receive:

- Your salesperson can bring you items from all over the store, without your having to leave the department or your dressing room.
- Getting other sizes for you saves time.

- Your salesperson will notify you when new merchandise arrives. The best selections of new inventory are often sold in this manner before they ever hit the floor for public display. This is especially true in the smaller boutiques and haberdasheries.

- Your salesperson will alert you to markdowns, before the price reductions are advertised. If possible, they may place a coveted item on hold for you or take a credit card number over the phone to make sure you get a créme-de-la-créme bargain.

Follow these eight "**Be**" guidelines to elicit the help of excellent salespeople. These methods work remarkably well in the smaller boutiques, as well as the large department stores.

1. **Be well dressed when you shop.** This is very important when you're attempting to gain the support of a salesperson; they should see dollar signs, as in sales coming their way, when they see you. Also, when they can observe your personal style and taste level, they can better serve you. If you go in looking ragged when you're shopping for quality business attire, they may not be inclined to run all over the store for you. They may bring you lower-quality, offbeat items because that is your nonverbal communication.

2. **Be an authentic shopper or act *as if*** — Try on clothes as if you were going to buy on that day. Buy something if possible and/or place a piece on hold for consideration. Thank the salesperson for helping you, ask for their card, and inquire about their days off. If they have regular hours, note those and their days off on their business card, right there in their presence.

3. **Be courteous.** Turn on the most captivating aspect of your personality. I did not say be phony; but, surely, *some* part of you can be genuinely charming and polite.

4. **Be sensitive** to their time and other customers they may be helping. Try on something else or browse around while they ring up a sale or finish with another customer. Don't portray a wimpy doormat in your demeanor, but assure them you will wait this time. If you show respect for their job and what they need to do to be successful, they will be more willing to add you to their special list.

5. Be supportive. Should you find an item in another department, take it to your befriended salesperson to purchase it. Support that person's individual sales record as much as you can. Send your friends to your salesperson for their purchases and tell them to mention your name.

6. Be loyal. Always ask for that particular person, but be nice to other salespeople in the department who may become your future servers/informers.

7. Be appreciative. Thank them for the excellent service they give you each time you interact with them. An expression of appreciation engenders more extraordinary service.

8. Be considerate. Do not take advantage of this person by constantly putting large numbers of items on hold, with no purchases, or by leaving a dressing room with clothes on the floor. Hang up the clothes you try on!

Return items only when absolutely necessary — high returns do not bode well for their sales records. If you want to exchange a size or get something else when returning an item, be sure that your appointed salesperson handles the transaction for you or he/she may lose credit for the original sale. Call ahead to make sure that she/he will be working during the hours you plan to make your exchange. The more loyalty you display, the more special favors they will be likely to do for you.

Part II. Bargain Shopping Par Excellence:

Four major rules dictate the art of finding spectacular bargains. Straying from these rules leads you to make mistakes, and wastes your time and money. Keep these rules in mind when you're bargain hunting.

Rules for Successful Bargain Shopping

1. A good deal does not always constitute a bargain.
2. Pre-shop in upscale stores first.
3. Differentiate between "Current Classics" and trendy fads.
4. QUALITY is a prime factor in gauging a bargain.

Rule 1: A good deal does not always constitute a bargain.

Beware of the *Good Deal Frenzy*. You may find a fabulous, high-quality designer garment for a fraction of its original cost, but it could look simply awful on you. Even if it looks just okay on you, this is not *your* bargain! You must always be true to yourself, to your coloring and body type, even when bargain shopping.

While you are building a wardrobe that empowers you, it is imperative that you embrace this guideline. Having done thousands of wardrobes, I can assure you those "good deals" that hang in your closet rarely worn — or that portray you unattractively — are not bargains, but an absolute waste of your money.

Some of my clients have been addicted to the unprofitable *Good-Deal Frenzy* until they go through my detox program. If you are hooked, consider becoming a Personal Shopper. You can specialize in bargain shopping and charge a fee for sniffing out good deals. If that prospect does not interest you, then you must unhook yourself from this defeatist behavior.

First, be ruthless in analyzing whether or not the item in question is right for you. If your Wow Meter does not register while you have it on, this is someone else's bargain, not yours. You are like a thief if you dare to buy someone else's empowerment, which is waiting for its rightful owner. *Bad Bargain Karma* will follow you for the rest of your days and your miracles — your bargain garments — will become harder and harder to find.

If you're still tempted to purchase that Good Deal even though you know in your heart that the piece does nothing to empower you, imagine yourself caught, arrested, and tried as a lowly shoplifter. Playing that mental game can take the edge off your craving to buy. Then walk away quickly. With this approach, you attract a genuine bargain to you — one that makes *you* look and feel like a million.

Rule 2: Pre-shop in upscale stores first.

Do your market research. Check out the inventories in stores that carry high-end merchandise *before* you dare to put even one foot in a discount store. Why? This trains your eye to recognize an authentic bargain. It is important to take even just a half hour to preview current styles and fabrics. Your eye will view discounted merchandise quite differently after a brief preview of fresh, new fashions. Stick to upscale department stores or smaller boutiques that have a reputation for quality.

Getting ahead means playing it smart and doing proper market research when you're bargain hunting for clothing. If you were shopping for a stereo or computer system, you would want to be informed on the latest technology available to maximize your potential long-term use; do the same with your wardrobe purchases. The *Painless Shopping Strategies* outlined in the previous section of this chapter (pages 200 – 212) also help to fine-tune your previewing skills.

Another advantage of checking out the newer merchandise before you discount shop is to increase your potential of finding real gems. Example: In one of my Image Consultants' Training Programs in San Francisco, I was teaching Rule 2 of Bargain Hunting. The exercises were designed to give trainees the correct tools to work with clients on a limited budget. First, we cruised through Neiman Marcus, Saks Fifth Avenue, and Macy's. Then we walked a few blocks away from Union Square to Loehman's, a renowned discount store. Within moments of entering Loehman's, we spotted a skirt that we had just seen at Neiman Marcus an hour before. Neiman's price was $275. At Loehman's, the very same skirt with the designer label still intact was priced at $60. We checked every inch of the skirt for flaws and found nothing. It was perfect — and it was priced $215 less than normal retail a few blocks away.

Why such a price variance? Often a designer cuts more pieces than are ordered wholesale from their retail vendors, or orders from market get canceled. Some designers will then approve the sale of their "extras" to discount buyers, such as Loehman's, Ross-Dress-For-Less, etc. for a radically low price just to recapture a part of their costs. (By the way, the skirt was innocuously hanging within racks of clothing billed as "New Arrivals.")

That same day, we also found a dress in the formal wear section that we had just seen *"on sale"* at Macy's. The price listed at Loehman's ($95) was still lower than the reduced sale price at Macy's, which had only only recently marked the dress down to $250 from the original price of $315. Because it passed all my quality standards, I bought the dress for my daughter. Knowing her body type well, I knew it would fit her perfectly and be flattering — an authentic gem of a bargain, because we had been looking for weeks for just that sort of stylish formal dress to add to her wardrobe.

Rule 3: Differentiate between "Current Classics" and trendy fads.

Being a slave to every fashion whim or trend is not what I advocate, even if money is no object. To be an effective bargain shopper, one must learn to discern between passing fads and classic styles in their updated versions. Fads come and go each season, but classics remain "in" with subtle changes about every five years. Trends are the bigger picture of our lifestyle changes, economy, etc. Trendy, faddish fashions arise from trends, but are in a different category from updated classics.

Example: Double-breasted jackets have been classic since the 1920s or before. They're still here and they're still considered classic, but they are a little different, driven by the trend toward a looser, relaxed fit. For men and women, they are slightly fuller and longer cut, especially in suiting and sport jackets for men. Even the sleeve length is worn longer than in the past. A late '90s "trendy fad" of this classic jacket would be a man's soft-shouldered style in a lime-green silk fabric — not a power business jacket, unless you own a nightclub in Los Angeles.

A current classic version for men would be a black or navy double-breasted jacket made of fine tropical wool, in the longer cut. This jacket is for Business Casual, Smart Casual, or dressy wear for both social and professional occasions. If you coveted the green silk jacket, get a lime-green or other brightly colored silk T-shirt to wear under your classic jacket to satisfy your trendy cravings.

An example for women is similar: Picture a longer-cut, slim jacket in a fine lightweight wool or silk in a neutral color like black, navy, taupe, or gray — or even a bright classic like red. The faddish version of this jacket would be in the same cut, but novelty-driven, with lots of silver or gold trim — or one made of shiny patent leather. Buy the plainer jacket that will mix with numerous outfits and take you any-where, professionally or socially. Then, if you so desire, add a metallic or shiny patent top or camisole underneath the jacket for a fun, trendy look when you're attending a social event.

Get the distinctions between "Trendy Fads" and "Current Classics"? Especially if you are slowly building an empowering wardrobe, it is very important that you stick to classics and not give in to those ever-changing fads.

Rule 4: QUALITY is a prime factor in gauging a bargain.

Your invisible Bargain Barometer is strengthened and finely tuned when you practice this guideline. Checkpoints for discerning real quali-ty are listed in the *Painless Shopping Strategies* section (pages 200 – 212). I urge you to do the exercises recommended. Become a quality connois-seur to find diamond bargains.

Take Pride in Your Bargain Hunting

There is absolutely no shame in seeking bargains in discount stores or even resale shops; they can be excellent sources for great finds. Remember to do your homework first and peruse new merchandise in an upscale store. Now that you know how to recognize quality, it's open season for bargain hunting. But where do you start? Where do you go for the best hunting? The following list of bargain hot spots and their "catch" brims over with helpful information to aid you in your quests.

Locating Hot Spots for Bargains — What's the Scoop?

■ Designer Outlet Stores

A shop stocked with a particular designer's merchandise at reduced prices. The designs are *usually* left over from last year. Generally, these stores offer the current season's wear. For instance: If it's late winter now, they will still be showing mostly winter clothing from last year.

Some designers manufacture, specifically for their outlet stores, styles that are never sold to regular retail vendors. There is nothing wrong with these designs, but you won't get the thrill of seeing your find at full price somewhere else.

Occasionally, the latest styles appear in outlet stores just a few weeks after their debut in the regular retail scene. Often, the best time to hit these stores is a few weeks *after* the initial season change. If you choose a recognized designer that consistently works with quality fabrics, these shops can be superb places to find basics at lower prices.

The Catch: Make sure your choices are not seconds. By this I mean slightly or seriously flawed garments that did not pass inspection for full-price retail wear. Check zippers, pleats, hems, seams, the fabric for pulled threads — in general, go over each piece with a Sherlock Holmes eye!

■ Discount Stores

Fun shopping because these stores generally offer all types of clothing from a wide range of designers. They buy their goods from retailers at the end of seasons and direct from designers and manufacturers all during the year. Authentic bargains do exist in these stores, but you must keep your eye well-honed for quality to find them. Another pitfall is falling into the trap of *only* shopping in these stores. If you do not follow Rule 2 and preview new styles first, your eye is easily deceived. You may end up never feeling or looking really up-to-date; you may look ordinary, instead of extraordinary.

I am not suggesting that you buy trendy apparel. To the contrary, buy updated classics. It is important to present yourself as currently living in the *now*, not ten years back. For instance, lapels on jackets change for men and women; button stances on men's jackets date the garment. Collar styles and skirt lengths can place you in one era or another. Know what you are buying!

The Catch: Be really thorough in checking these garments for flaws because much of their inventory is made up of seconds. Avoid tired garments, regardless of what terrific price tags they may display. Much of the merchandise has been tried on thousands of times (literally) and has been shipped from here to there many times. All this handling is wearing on the fabrics, diluting their fresh crispness. Remember, tired fabrics make you appear tired and ragged — a waste of your money. Be sure to check the return policy in these stores. Few have full refund policies. Many have none at all, with all sales final. Most will only give you a store credit if the items are returned within seven days.

■ Resale Shops

In upscale resale shops, you can find amazing bargains. The key is to shop in high-end neighborhoods, in upscale shops only, to find quality, not-too-outdated clothing and accessories. These resale shops have a firm policy to accept only apparel in excellent condition that is less than two years old. The only exceptions are couture-quality, classically time-less designer pieces that are like new regardless of their age.

Inventories are filled by consignment contracts with individuals. Able to buy new fashions each change of season, many people take their past season's apparel to an upscale resale shop. This shows an evolved consciousness because it is a form of recycling and actually aids the pocketbooks of many. It is not uncommon to find garments with the original price tag still on them, obviously never worn.

If you have a yen for a designer look at a fraction of retail costs, check out the *finest* resale shop in your city. For instance, you could enjoy the warmth of a stunning cashmere topcoat for pennies compared to retail prices. If you need formal wear and you have only a few dollars to spend, check out some excellent resale shops. The socially elite attend many formal functions, and you can often find fabulous bargains on black-tie outfits worn only once or twice.

The Catch: Only shop for resale goods in an extremely upscale store. Most often these are found in the more elite neighborhoods or shopping areas. Otherwise, you run the risk of getting clothing that is so old that it has already been outdated for many years. The lower-end shops are not going to be as discriminating about the merchandise they accept.

Occasionally, you do find a garment that has never been worn, but usually items in all resale stores are used clothing. It is my personal belief that fabrics can absorb the feelings of the wearer. If you are an extremely sensitive soul, this may not be for you. However, many of these items have actually not been tried on and handled as much as some of the pieces in discount stores. If you are on an extremely tight budget, these stores are worth checking out. Generally, all sales are final, with no exchanges or credits. Choose carefully.

■ Sales at Major Department Stores or Boutiques

These are overlooked by many people, but they offer some of the best bargain hunting ever — you just need to be informed *prior* to its open season to cash in. All major department stores have a markdown schedule they follow each fashion season. So the store can recapture costs and make room for their flow of new merchandise, prices are reduced on their older inventory that was not sold that season. I use the word "older" here only to distinguish previously received merchandise; typically, the sale items are not old, outdated garments.

The point: You can *always* expect to find some items reduced at any given time in the larger department stores. You may have to look in every nook and cranny because they are often found in out-of-the-way places marked by obscure signs. The newer, full-price merchandise gets display prominence at the beginning of each fashion season. Toward the middle of the season, the first markdowns begin. Later, with further reductions, there is a major sale event. You want to be informed about the initial and later markdowns the very second the reduced prices are available, whether or not you can buy at that time. Generally, the markdowns are staggered. At a major sale, there may be merchandise marked at 25 percent off, some at 50 percent off, and even some at 75 percent off.

The pick of the best bargains is found *before* any advertising appears. If you're not a member of the preferred customer clubs (those who regularly spend sizable sums in that store), how can you be privy to this valuable information? Establish a relationship with a leading salesperson and she/he will call you as your favorite items are being reduced. Generally, aggressive salespeople will phone you prior to markdowns or special events. It is to your advantage to encourage this. Be a disciple of the eleven commandments listed in the Painless Shopping Strategies. *Command Extraordinary Service* (pages 210 – 212) tells you how to successfully enroll a salesperson in your bargain pursuits. Reread this section (and follow its guidelines)to be privy to Sacred Sale Information prior to public advertising.

The Department Store Catch: Beware of sales marked as "Special Purchases." Sometimes, this is when a store brings in items apart from their normal inventory just for the sale. Generally, this merchandise is priced higher than its actual value, then marked down to look like a major reduction in price. In most cases, the so-called reduced price is near what the item would retail for anyway — not a good deal. Usually there are posted signs noting "Special Purchase" to mark this kind of inventory. Normally, it is the larger department stores and smaller chains that engage in these deceptive sale practices. Rarely have I seen a locally owned shop or a small boutique do this; nonetheless, be alert.

Also, it is a good idea to check the return policy on sale merchandise in department stores and the smaller shops. *Always* ask! For some sale events a store may change their regular policy and revert to "all sales final" on reduced items. When making your selections, it's best to know what your options are. Can you make exchanges? Return for money back? Return for store credit? Or if you change your mind when you're home, are you just stuck with your choice?

■ **Department Store Discount Stores**: High-end stores like Saks Fifth Avenue and Neiman Marcus now have discount stores to sell the merchandise that did not sell in their regular stores. These are excellent sources for bargains. Follow the same rules and cautions as for other bargain shopping.

PART III.   CASUAL MIRACLES:

A magnificent wardrobe can be yours. You can be powerfully dressed for any occasion, with astute planning. McSly would never want you to know, but you can accomplish this fete on *ANY* budget, even a shoestring budget. How? Follow seven simple steps to enjoy the rewards of such a wardrobe.

Step 1: Decide it.

To accomplish any goal, you must first decide you *want* it, whatever that particular end result may be. This is just like ordering from a menu. Have you ever gone to a restaurant absolutely starving and been immediately served the moment you were seated? Regardless of how hungry you may be, you must first decide what you want — and you must place the order.

Deciding is the fundamental step in *having*. Decide now to own a casual wardrobe that empowers you to get ahead!

- If money is no object for you, follow the Painless Shopping Strategies and read the *Power Casual Essentials* chapters. (For women, Chapter 5, page 111; for men, Chapter 6, page 147.) Then have fun buying several Power Casual outfits.

- If you have budget concerns, master the basic "How-To" of building a Power Casual wardrobe. Remain connected to your decision and your desire to have casual clothing that gives you the edge.

The great philosopher, Goethe, spoke of the unleashing of a miraculous power by simply making a genuine commitment. If you firmly decide to have empowering casual clothing, you may be amazed at the events and unexpected happenings that begin to take place in your life. Improbable bargains, raises, or gifts. The possibilities are endless.

DECISION HOLDS MAGIC.

Goethe said:

> Until one is committed there is hesitancy,
> the chance to draw back...always ineffectiveness.
> Concerning all acts of initiative (and creation),
> there is one elementary truth, the ignorance of which
> kills countless ideas and splendid plans:
> that the moment one definitely commits oneself,
> then providence moves too. All sorts of things
> occur to help one that would *never* have occurred.
> A whole stream of events issues from the decision,
> raising in one's favor all manner of unforeseen incidents,
> meetings and material assistance, which no man could
> have dreamt would have come his way.

This may seem too simple to be true, but I can attest to the power of these words. An entire book could be written based on the miracles I have experienced merely through the act of committing. I will share one incident with you.

Several years ago, I fell in love with an expensive line of designer shoes, *Manolo Blahnik*. At the time my income was greatly reduced because I was spending much of my time caring for my father who was terminally ill with cancer. While I did need a new pair of black pumps, it was not in my budget to spend $400 for couture shoes. The price tag reflected fine leather, high-design detailing, and quality workmanship, but it was unduly inflated due to the exclusive designer's name printed on the inside.

As I stood in the Neiman Marcus in Houston, admiring the beauty and fine quality of this particular shoe, I reminded myself of the commitment I had made to myself some years back — to only buy high-quality, well-made shoes. From every angle, I peered at the design features of this particular shoe, absorbing the feeling of the superb leather. Silently, I made a commitment that someday I would buy this designer's shoes. The feeling traveled all the way down to my toes. My feet believed me.

On the following day, during the three-hour drive back to Austin (from Houston), the Neiman Marcus Last Call store flashed into my mind several times. Even though I was pressed for time, I decided to stop by there before going back to the office. (For those of you who aren't familiar with a *Last Call* store, it is an outlet where already-marked-down inventory from a regular Neiman Marcus is sold at further reductions.)

Upon entering the Austin store that morning, I noticed a flurry of people near the back. Much to my delight, I had arrived when a new shipment of shoes had just arrived. A Preferred Customer Sale was in progress — prior to advertising to the general public. Guess what I found? There in a size 7M was the exact pair of *Manolo Blahnik* black heels I had so coveted the day before. And they were not the original price of $400. Instead, this pair displayed the miraculous price of $120. And they were in perfect condition! (Yes, I bought them.)

Curious about the store policy that would allow for my miracle, the next time I was in Houston, I went by the regular Neiman Marcus and talked to one of the shoe salesmen. Joe helped me put my puzzle together. Basically, this was the scoop: The shoe I had admired in the store was part of the new fall collection, even though it was a repeat from the spring line. My miracle shoe was actually part of the spring inventory. As a spring shoe, the black leather had not sold very well. A few pairs were still in stock after the three usual markdowns. Store policy is such that the older merchandise is shipped out to the *Last Call* outlets when it has not sold in the final markdowns at the end of each season. Even if the shoe is identical to ones coming in with the new collection, it gets marked down, based on the date it came in originally. Then, if after all the markdowns it still has not sold, it is shipped to *Last Call*.

I bought the shoe in early September for one-third the original price. The *Last Call* salesperson said that my shoe was one of two pairs received in that style — a size 7 in black and a size 9 in dark brown. Had I not stopped by that particular morning, I would have missed my miracle.

It may seem that luck smiled on me that day or that it was sheer coincidence that I stopped by *Last Call* at that particular hour. I do not believe it was a fluke. The commitment I made the day before was the reason the urge to go by *Last Call* at that particular time was so compelling — and I listened to and acted upon my inner feeling.

If you want to increase the number of opportunities for miracles to come your way, reread Goethe's statement. Carefully absorb each word. Test the theory in your own way. First and foremost, be committed to your own success. Keep in mind that quality attire can give you an edge in your attempts to get ahead. Make a genuine commitment to wear *only* empowering casual clothing.

Step 2: Believe it.

Believe that you can and will own the wardrobe you want, regardless of how limiting your budget may be. If you are on an anorexic budget, this is a critical step because it is here that your personal saboteur will attempt to trick you into disbelieving.

Nietzsche, another great philosopher, said: *"All great change occurs in silence."* Observe what you are thinking and verbalizing about your future new clothes. If you hear yourself saying any words about not being able to afford world-class clothing, immediately change the negative message into a believing, positive statement. Discipline your mind and tongue with corrective declarations if you catch yourself saying or thinking thoughts that betray your goal.

Step 3: See it.

Support your belief and commitment with visualizations. In your mind's eye, visualize "you" wearing Power Casual attire. You may be thinking, *"I am just no good at that — I can't visualize anything."* Seeing detail in the mind's eye does not come easily to many people. The following activities facilitate this process.

> • Cut out pictures of Power Casual clothing that appeals to you. Catalogues and magazines are a good source. Keep *the chosen ones* in a file folder or glue them into a blank book.

Look at them regularly, lavishing each one with your attention, intention, and desire. Simple? Yes, and very important. Your subconscious mind is a powerful instrument. Without judging or prioritizing, it responds to images that you impress upon it; then it seeks to bring those images into your everyday reality. This is why people often get what they fear the most.

Cut out pictures of the clothing items that you really like and definitely want to own. If you look with attentive focus at these pictures daily, you will get either the exact items pictured or strong similarities. "Viewing with attentive focus" means to project your mind into the images. Try to feel those particular garments and fabrics on YOU, on your body. Imagine what you would do when wearing them and how you would behave in them. Let yourself enjoy the feeling of this process. In these fantasy moments, act and feel as if the items in the pictures are already yours.

Music can expedite accessing your feeling nature. Positive emotion helps to imprint a clear, strong image in the depths of your subconscious mind. Put some of your favorite music on to help you really get into this exercise. This works only if you work it!

• Go into several stores and shop for your desired items. Time well spent, this activity supports your goals. Try on some pieces — preferably complete outfits — to SEE how you look. Observe all the nuances and details. This step facilitates your visualizing processes and serves to further imprint clothing images upon your psyche.

Equally significant in this imprint is the experience of how quality, empowering garments FEEL to you — to your body. Allow yourself to relish the *feel* of fine fabrics against your skin. If you fall in love with an item, ask a salesperson to please phone you when it goes on sale. Expecting future sales, an organized salesperson will happily comply.

Step 4: Buy basics in your best power-neutral color.

Power colors are always dark in tone. Power neutrals are black, navy, gray, charcoal, and brown — with the best business choices being navy, black, and dark gray. Select the power-neutral color that most flatters your skin tone and the one that makes you *feel* powerful. For many, black and navy both look great, but usually there is one color that pops for them. They can feel the difference in their own confidence and power by putting on that color. For me, it is black. Even though navy looks good on me, I do not connect as easily with my own sense of magic when wearing navy as I do with black.

Every serious businessperson should have at least one suit or jacket in solid black, navy, or dark gray to coordinate with their other existing pieces. Solid-colored garments are preferred. Working with one color family when first building your wardrobe also simplifies accessorizing. This strategy means you need fewer shoes, belts, and jewelry.

Step 5: Commit to acquiring one garment a month.

Regardless of a restrictive budget, you must be committed to adding one garment or accessory every month to successfully build a wardrobe. Even microbudgets usually have some room to cut corners — like forgoing that dessert with lunch, not eating out as often, or whatever frivolities you have a penchant for. Even five to ten dollars here and there in your "Clothing Kitty" can add up quickly.

Reread Goethe's statement. Only with a genuine commitment can your miracles find you. Expect miracles *and* do your part by having a Power Casual Savings Plan. Practice the Rules for Successful Bargain Shopping (page 212). And remember, *quality over quantity*. Of course, if you can afford more than one fabulous garment or accessory one month, then certainly go for it.

Step 6: Buy *only* high-quality items.

Buy only current classic styles, only garments that look superb on YOU, only garments that make you feel like you're worth millions. Buy this type of apparel to enjoy the benefits of a long-term relationship with clothes that help you get ahead.

Classic garments in quality fabrics are timeless. How you put them together changes with current trends, but the basic styling remains the same. Example: A black turtleneck sweater in cashmere or other fine wool has been classic for decades. In the '60s, one would not consider wearing such a fine garment with jeans. However, today it is considered chic to mix dressier pieces, especially black, with denim.

Step 7: Buy according to the Capsule Wardrobe plan.

Study the Capsule Wardrobe plan outlined in Chapter 4 (see page 94). Consisting of a few essential garments that work well together, the Capsule Wardrobe is a delight for a tight budget. Buy only according to a specific plan until you have two complete capsules hanging in your closet.

The same jacket, trousers, or skirt can be worn several times in one week. If it looks extraordinary on you, this is especially true while you're in building mode. To wear items repeatedly, your garments must exude top quality and be in neutral colors. Because of its pared-down nature, a Capsule Wardrobe always demands quality. *Remember — looking terrific attracts dollars and more great clothing to you!*

"Don't fight forces,
use them."

— Buckminster Fuller

The Power of Gravity

If you are still skeptical about the benefits of a Power Casual image, here's a question for you: Do you have to believe in gravity for its force to affect your life? No — if you're knocked off balance when you're riding a bike, you and the bike are coming down.

Gravity doesn't have a casual attitude. It always operates at full power, whether it's night or day, hot or cold, rainy or sunny. To win — and to stay on top — always power up when you dress down!

"People do not simply form impressions, they get anchored to them. Even more important, people with little time — almost all people today — are apt to make first impressions as snap judgments, and then base all their later decisions on them. First impressions have never been more critical — they take hold very quickly, and they become the anchors to which you and your success are tied."

— Harry Beckwith, *Selling the Invisible*

"All truth goes though three steps. First, it is ridiculed. Second, it is violently opposed. Finally, it is accepted as self-evident."   — Arthur Schopenhauer

To continue to develop your personal power, log on to:

www.casualpower.com

The Casual Power web site will be updated regularly with new information and illustrations. We invite you to send your questions to the "Casually Ask Sherry" column on the web site. Also send us your success stories, your McSly discoveries, and your worst casual casualties.

Sherry Maysonave and her team of consultants are available for speaking engagements, corporate workshops, private seminars, and personal consultations. If you would like information about the services offered by Empowerment Enterprises, check the "Professional Services" pages of the website, www.casualpower.com, or call 512.370.9575.

Empowerment Enterprises Mission Statement:

We are devoted to assisting others attain professional and personal success. Our communication programs and image services are custom designed to empower the individual or group, however unique, to easily achieve their goals. It is our belief that success increases your quality of life, your sphere of influence, and your ability to make a positive difference for others.

Our philosophy and presentation style is motivating, educational, and inspiring. We recognize the three different learning modalities (visual, audio, and kinesthetic) and we strive to include aspects of each mode in our dynamic, interactive courses and consultations.